The
Psychodynamic
approach to therapeutic change

Sage Therapeutic Change Series

Books in the *Sage Therapeutic Change Series* examine 'change' as the goal of counselling and psychotherapy. Each book takes a different therapeutic approach and looks at how change is conceptualised and worked with by practitioners from that approach. Giving examples which demonstrate how theory and principles are put into practice, the books are suitable for both trainee and experienced counsellors and psychotherapists.

Series Editor: Windy Dryden

Books in the series:

The Rational Emotive Behavioural Approach to Therapeutic Change
Windy Dryden & Michael Neenan

The Psychodynamic Approach to Therapeutic Change
Rob Leiper & Michael Maltby

The Person-Centred Approach to Therapeutic Change
Michael McMillan

The
Psychodynamic
approach to therapeutic change

Rob Leiper
and
Michael Maltby

SAGE Publications
London • Thousand Oaks • New Delhi

First published 2004

 SAGE Publications Ltd
1 Oliver's Yard
55 City Road
London EC1Y 1SP

SAGE Publications Inc.
2455 Teller Road
Thousand Oaks, California 91320

SAGE Publications India Pvt Ltd
B-42, Panchsheel Enclave
Post Box 4109
New Delhi 100 017

British Library Cataloguing in Publication data

A catalogue record for this book is available from the British
Library

ISBN 0 7619 4870 8
ISBN 0 7619 4871 6 (pbk)

Library of Congress Control Number: 2003109259

Typeset by C&M Digitals (P) Ltd, Chennai, India
Printed in Great Britain by TJ International Ltd, Padstow, Cornwall

To our wives, Rose and Tove – forces for change.

Contents

List of Boxes, Tables and Figures

Boxes

History and Theory:

Case Example:

Tables

Figures

This is a book about change in psychodynamic psychotherapy. It puts change at the centre of the therapeutic enterprise and explores how the process of change can be understood from a variety of perspectives within the psychodynamic tradition. These extend from the ideas of Freud to the radical developments in thought that are occurring in the present era. Although there is no definitive model of change in psychodynamic theory, the book provides a structure for integrating a diversity of approaches into a coherent overall framework. We have found that this framework has clinical utility and provides an effective means of introducing the theory and practice of contemporary psychodynamic work. It has the merit of being accessible but also – by taking a progressive approach – enables the genuine complexity of the issues to be engaged with in increasing depth.

We have divided the book into three parts. Part I examines the concept of change from a dynamic point of view (Chapter 1), and provides a broad outline of the nature and development of psychodynamic theory (Chapter 2). Part II (Chapters 3–8) presents the core framework of change processes in terms of six general themes. These chapters attempt to interweave theory and practice in a cumulative fashion to build an integrated picture of how change takes place in psychodynamic therapy. Part III locates therapeutic change in relation to a number of wider social contexts (Chapter 9) and concludes by proposing an overall vision of a spiral of change (Chapter 10). A number of boxes and tables supplement the text. These contain additional theoretical and historical summaries to help meet the needs of different readers. We have also included a continuous case example that spans the central six chapters of the book to illustrate some of the processes discussed.

We hope that the book will be of interest to a wide audience. It is aimed towards those trying to come to grips with the daunting range of psychodynamic ideas for the first time but offers an integrative model for thinking about change that should also be stimulating and useful for more experienced practitioners.

Our thanks are due to Karen Hinchcliffe and Wendy Rosser for their assistance with typing and layout. Also to David Sperlinger, Rosemary Kent, Celia Hunt and Maria Maltby for their willingness to read and provide feedback on work in progress. Needless to say, in keeping with the spirit of the book, we must take responsibility for the changes that we've made!

Rob Leiper
Michael Maltby

PART I
Change and Psychodynamic Psychotherapy

The idea of change is fundamental to all the psychotherapies – it is their reason for being. However, from the point of view of psychodynamic therapy, change is not a straightforward issue. As an approach it is acutely sensitive to the difficulties, complexities and paradoxes that beset the therapeutic enterprise. Psychodynamic theory is distinguished by its vision of human life as problematic and conflictual – and this is no less true of therapy. In seeking to promote change, few things are pure and simple.

This outlook is true of psychodynamic theory itself. It is characterised by different perspectives and competing models. It has also changed in many ways in the course of its evolution. The complexities of the issues that it addresses are reflected in the intricate and sometimes elusive conceptualisations to which it has given birth. What they hold in common is the idea that individuals exist in a state of tension with themselves, other people and the world in general. The development of the psyche and of emotional difficulties has its foundation in the ways in which this struggle is worked out. It is this 'dynamic' character that marks human existence and which suggests that although change is the business of therapy, it is not an idea that can be taken for granted. In a sense, change is as problematic as staying the same!

The aim of therapeutic change

What exactly counts as 'change' in psychotherapy? At first sight this might seem unproblematic. As a therapy its aim must be healing and the alleviation of suffering through the removal of the symptoms or problems that lead people to seek help. Psychodynamic therapy arose out of this 'medical model' of change: the aim was the removal of symptoms through the correction of their underlying pathology. As the complexities of psychological change became clearer so too did the problems of maintaining this vision of the psychotherapeutic process.

One difficulty is establishing exactly what the end point of change, its goal and so its direction, might be. 'Normality' has a poor reputation these days with its overtones of social control and intolerance of difference. Other terms, such as 'maturity' or 'mental health' fare little better.

Fleshing out the details of such ideals is only possible within a particular socio-cultural situation and its context of values. For his part, Freud famously referred to the ability 'to love and to work'. However, the psychodynamic tradition has been reluctant to stay at the level of external rather than inner – psychological – descriptors of change. One reason is its therapeutic focus on subjectivity and the inner world of experience. But there has also been the belief that external behavioural criteria of change are typically too specific, localised and perhaps minor to be the most important therapeutic goals. They are seen as superficial in relation to the diffuse and extensive difficulties for which people commonly seek psychotherapeutic help. There is a wish by many therapists and clients to look deeper – to seek more fundamental 'structural' change in the personality.

An important reason for seeking structural change is the idea that in addition to being more pervasive, it will also be more permanent. Change in relatively superficial behaviour patterns is thought likely to be temporary, vulnerable to changing circumstances and subject to reversal. Although therapeutic changes can be rapid, even dramatic, psychodynamic therapists have come to suspect that rapid progress can also be unstable and almost equally transient. Efforts have thus been focused on working steadily for the long term. Even short-term psychodynamic therapies seek to start a process of development that is consolidated on a longer time scale. Such gradual progress, however, is not necessarily built incrementally and continuously. Because a dynamic vision suggests that psychological structure is a delicate balance of competing forces, the process of change is not likely to be linear: it involves reversals and regressions, plateaux with little progress and sudden breakthroughs to a qualitatively different level. Indeed, one definition of psychological 'pathology' might be when this balance is maintained in a rigid, inflexible way. The ability to change, to respond flexibly to life's circumstances in adaptive and creative ways is probably a good psychodynamic definition of a healthy state of being. The capacity for further change thus becomes the goal of change in psychotherapy!

There is high ambition in these aims of enduring structural change which has meant that psychodynamic thinking has always been drawn to the grand themes of life: personal transformation, fundamental meaning, creation and destruction, birth and death, even the origins of society. Therapies with a more modest outlook typically take a more pragmatic view and build their theories to serve more restricted ends. But this grappling with the major issues in human life is one of the strengths and the attractions of the psychodynamic outlook: it attempts to encompass a vision of life. This vision – along with the definitions of psychological structure in which it is framed – varies greatly between theorists. For Freud it had quite an austere aspect: maturity is about facing what is painful and unacceptable in ourselves; our problems are not just about bad things happening to us but about our own questionable motives; life is intrinsically problematic and unsatisfactory and we should value above all such virtues as restraint, patience, fortitude and unflinching honesty. This stoical element in Freud's vision (we might say in his character) is represented in his well-known comment to a patient that much would be gained if they transformed her 'hysterical misery into common unhappiness' (Breuer and Freud, 1895: 305).

However, this vision can be translated into aims that seem less bleak. Indeed, Freud did go on to suggest to his patient that she could become 'better armed against the unhappiness'. The emotional repertoire that enables someone to lead life well includes acceptance of the wishful, painful and conflictual aspects of our personalities, so that we can become better friends with ourselves (and so with others). It also involves finding a new immediacy and intensity in living and better ways of dealing with life's continuing challenges. Psychological difficulty arises from the avoidance of these problems in living in ways that stultify our own potential. Psychotherapy's aim, then, is to enable us to develop capacities that free our potential for inventiveness and pleasure in life.

In articulating these ambitious goals for itself, the psychodynamic tradition seems to have swayed between optimism and pessimism. Particularly in the early days there was an idealised vision of what could be achieved by the processes of psychotherapy and the knowledge gained from it. Towards the end of his career Freud (1937) had formed a more pessimistic view: the intractable difficulties in human life and our frailties as individuals made psychoanalysis (together with those other specialisms in human change, education and government) an 'impossible profession', always destined to achieve unsatisfactory results. Perhaps this ironic comment is best taken as a necessary corrective to the tendency – still present – to idealise any form of psychotherapy.

The tasks of psychotherapy

From the psychodynamic point of view, most emotional suffering is extensively and intricately connected, in ways that the person does not perceive, to other aspects of the way they live. This challenges any simple view of personal problems and how to change them. It also alerts us to the ambivalence that people generally have about changing. Someone in pain of course wants to be free of it and of the restrictions by which they feel trapped. But people also fear change: they fear the loss of security and familiarity in what they know. In coming into therapy, they often fear losing themselves and becoming someone else. Attention to this element of unwillingness and difficulty with change – the client's 'ambivalence' and 'resistance' – alerts us to an ambiguity in understanding what she[1] (or anyone) wants. Since much of this ambivalence and resistance is not directly in the field of awareness – is 'unconscious' – these obscure and contradictory motives will inevitably be brought into therapy. The client wants 'help' to be sure but what exactly is that in her mind? There is a profound irony that because of the way unconscious motives are brought into the therapeutic situation, the kind of help that clients imagine getting from a therapist often turns out to be just more of the same old stuff! The problems which they want solved are replicated in the way they imagine them being tackled: someone who tends to depend too much on others for direction seeks a confident advisor; someone who is cut off from their feelings and over-intellectualises seeks an expert to discuss things with, and so on. Thus in the psychodynamic view, while change may be on offer, it is usually not – and should not be – quite what the client may think is needed. Nor indeed should the therapist presume to know what it should be. Exactly what will be helpful remains to be discovered in the course of the therapeutic work.

While this may reflect appropriate humility, it leaves the therapist in an uncertain position with regard to her role as an agent of change. The solution to this has been a radical one: the fundamental stance of the therapist should not be to try to 'cure' or directly change the client. Psychodynamic therapy is not a 'repair shop' in which people are straightened out. Instead, the task is to seek understanding – to attempt to describe rather than to alter things directly. If a client's awareness is extended, it is reasoned, this increases her freedom and capacity to choose. If a therapist actively seeks change, this offers a vision which functions as a demanding ideal: some bits of the client are good, others bad (which is, of course, what most clients already feel). In some psychoanalytic thinking this approach has been taken to extremes. It has been suggested that the therapist should have no aim other than to 'analyse' – change is just a by-product. In a sense, this is a piece of wise nonsense. Underlying it is the appreciation that a preoccupation with aims can hinder effectiveness. The therapist must not *need* (rather than hope) to help the client. On a session-to-session basis, not being beset by therapeutic ambition enables the therapist to find the appropriate state of mind, one in which she is not confused by and drawn in to what *one* part of the client may insist is wanted.

This stance places a premium on the responsibility of the client. Psychodynamic therapy attempts (in spite of some past tendencies to the contrary) to enable clients to retell their story in terms of the intentions they have and the choices they make. Of course, most forms of psychotherapy are premised on the value of clients taking responsibility for their lives and the need for therapists not to impose their own values. The difference in the psychodynamic approach is its special sensitivity to the ways in which therapists do in fact influence clients and, crucially, the ways in which clients will lead therapists to take responsibility for their difficulties. The therapeutic approach thus endeavours to embody a deep respect for the client's autonomy, something that is fostered by the therapist's reflective rather than directive stance, sometimes at the cost of considerable frustration for the client! The therapist tries not to relieve the

client of her responsibility by leaving the possibilities for change a.
as she can.

Nevertheless taken to an extreme, the notion of having no aims ↺
responsibility for change is rather a defensive point of view that can be
used to deny legitimate questions about the effectiveness and appropriateness of a dynamic or 'analytic' approach to a therapeutic need. There
are different levels of aim and a constant interaction between them. A
vision of a long-term outcome for this client – who she might potentially
become – is always somewhere in the therapist's mind and it is futile to
pretend to dispense with it (Sandler and Dreher, 1995). It inevitably
informs the 'process' decisions of what to do and say in particular sessions and the more specific process aims that lie behind them. As psychodynamic therapy developed there was an increasing emphasis on these
process considerations; principally because experience taught that the
means were as important as the ends and, to effect lasting change, the
ends could rarely be approached directly.

Change and the process of therapy

The overall format of therapeutic practice encompassed within the psychodynamic tradition is enormously variable. It extends from brief once
weekly therapies (10–25 sessions), or even consultations of just a few
sessions, through to intensive long-term work, with several sessions a
week extending over many years. Clearly, the therapeutic aims should be
appropriate to whatever constraints may be imposed by the client, the
therapist's training or the context of practice. A distinction is commonly
made here between analysis and therapy. However, this is a demarcation
that is often driven by professional politics and issues of status. The criteria suggested to define the difference turn out to vary greatly. External
markers are the intensity and length of the expected contract and the use
of a couch as opposed to face-to-face seating. More 'internal', process-
oriented criteria have also been proposed, particularly the rigour with which
the therapist holds to a neutral, interpretative posture rather than pursu-
ing some form of explicit therapeutic change. Other internal criteria suggest
that it is the quality of the client's engagement with the therapist in the task
of self-understanding that is crucial. The nature of the relationship and the
therapeutic atmosphere that particular client/therapist pairs construct
between them varies considerably whether or not they meet these criteria.
We consider the analysis/therapy distinction rather unhelpful, indeed
untenable in practice. All therapeutic contracts seek change. Goals vary in
ambition and different individuals require different 'techniques' to achieve
them, so the therapist's posture needs to adjust depending on a whole range
of factors. Some judgements about what is appropriate can be made more or
less easily and reliably early in the therapy, and so affect the form of the
initial contract; others only emerge in the experience of working together.

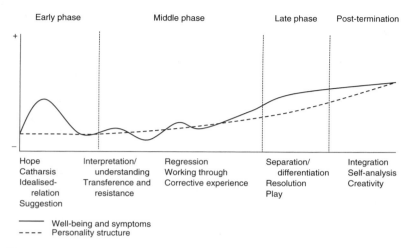

Figure 1.1 Idealised course of psychodynamic psychotherapy (adapted from Wolberg, 1977)

For the purposes of getting an overview it is possible to propose what might be called an average expectable course of therapy, with particular issues associated with different phases of the work (see Figure 1.1). At the start of most therapies, there are a number of non-specific influences that make for an encouraging and supportive experience. These include: the hope of relief, an idealised relationship with the therapist, an element of 'suggestion' in the implication that all will be well, and the relief provided by emotional expression. Some clients leave during this first flush of well-being and some, with their own energy remobilised, may maintain that improvement. But no underlying change will have taken place. For those who continue, this honeymoon period will end sooner or later: the problems recur. The therapist is not as wonderful as previously thought, the commitment is a lot to ask and so on. If the client sticks with it at this point, the real work begins.

As the client's ambivalence and resistance to self-awareness and change emerges explicitly and is confronted, it is quite likely that old (or new) problems will erupt. Anxiety or depression increase and the experience of being involved in a real and painful struggle has to be borne. If the client drops out in this middle phase she is likely to feel little benefit. The therapist provokes changes by disturbing the client's usual patterns of relating and of understanding herself. To be affected by the therapy she needs in some degree to be unsettled, challenged, even shocked. It is this that gives rise to the old saying that you have to get worse before you can get better. Crises and breakdowns in the accustomed ways of being are looked to as opportunities to break through to a new more flexible level of equilibrium. Disturbance is necessary – but not too much; the client also needs support from the therapist in order to bear it. However, in psychodynamic work, by challenging defences and enabling clients to confront themselves, the therapist inevitably stimulates some emotional pain.

If the work proceeds well, all the psychodynamic processes of change with which this book is concerned may come into play. The client enlarges her experience in a way that enables her to understand and master emotions, widening her choices and supporting her to give up old securities and the fringe benefits of her 'illness' to experiment with new forms of relating, to herself and to others. In the final phases, the client must start to give up the dependence that she may have developed on the therapist and deal with issues of separation and loss, hopefully internalising not only specific understandings gained but the processes of self-awareness and self-containment. Indeed, the process of change is not finished with the end of therapy. The personal capabilities that have been acquired can consolidate and further extend in their subsequent influence on life-experience.

Of course, no specific therapy should be expected to follow such an idealised course. It is not useful to homogenise the psychodynamic therapies in all their variety into an imagined single process. However, spelling out this simplified model of therapeutic progress enables us to see the work as a whole, something which is not always easy to do when in the midst of it. Even short-term therapies typically pass through a number of phases not dissimilar to this, albeit in a compressed form.

The client's experience

The client's experience of therapy, as might be anticipated from the process outlined above, is rarely easy or smooth. She might well feel a good deal of puzzlement or frustration that the therapist does not respond to her in the ways that she would have expected. The client might have hoped for more comfort and reassurance than seems to be forthcoming. It might even seem as though the therapist has answers that are wilfully withheld. Even as new understandings of her situation emerge, she is left to decide what to do with them rather than receiving the guidance that is often hoped for. Indeed, her very hopes for change might be held up for questioning. It can be a disorienting experience – and it can get worse!

As accustomed ways of handling distress, avoiding disturbing experiences and bolstering shaky self-esteem are challenged and the light of awareness is focused on previously obscure aspects of both past and present experience, the client is faced with what is often thought of as her own 'demons' – the things she fears most. Unpleasant emotional states and traumatic memories may be uncovered, fond illusions unmasked. She may have to face some very difficult feelings – including her own 'nastiness'.

Indeed, these problematic experiences may come alive in the therapeutic relationship itself. A strand of disappointment can also run through the work: high hopes of a whole new life prove illusory; a final answer to the question of who she is proves unforthcoming. She has to face what therapy cannot remove: the real difficulties and uncertainty of living.

Of course, it is possible to overemphasise the ways in which psychotherapy hurts. The process can go more smoothly; exploration and discovery are often felt to be rewarding; at times it is even fun! The benefits of the work can accrue quite quickly and result in welcome and encouraging life changes. Those benefits can eventually be profound (although not necessarily dramatic). Clients may feel that they understand and cope better with symptoms, even in those instances where they don't disappear. More generally, there is an improved capacity for self-management, together with an increase in self-knowledge and self-acceptance. Clients report the relief of feeling more ordinary, of recognising and accepting their own limits (as well as those of therapy and the therapist). They have more confidence in accepting the good things in life and develop a capacity to negotiate conflicts both within themselves and in their relationships. They are better able to consider their impact on other people and their part in it when difficulties arise. In putting their experiences into words they are able to articulate a more coherent version of who they are in relation to their own history and unfolding circumstances. They develop a sense of 'becoming' (Martin and Holloway, 2002).

The therapist's experience

It should be clear that the process of psychodynamic therapy is expected to be intrinsically difficult as well as rewarding. In fact, this is true for both parties: the therapeutic enterprise can be emotionally testing and at times even painful for the therapist. The therapeutic stance is very demanding, requiring as it does a combination of emotional involvement and empathic closeness with an element of distance and questioning, even scepticism, towards the client's accounts of herself. It is difficult simply not to do the natural thing when faced with someone who is suffering. It requires confidence in the therapeutic approach and a willingness to stick with it when facing resistance. At one level, as with all therapies, there is a close involvement with the distress and often despair that the client brings: the therapist has to survive this. But more than that, she has to go deeper into it, to challenge the client's ways of defending herself and in effect to provoke more pain. This goes against the therapist's human impulse to want to make things better. Indeed, people who become therapists are likely to feel this desire more than most: it typically goes to the roots of their own personality and motivation. The process almost inevitably raises all of the therapist's own self-doubts and she must come to terms with and contain the issues which this stirs up in her. In fact the work of a psychodynamic therapist is profoundly self-referential: we are not different from our clients; we struggle with the same emotional difficulties as they do. As a result, we are likely also to be changed time and again through the experience of working therapeutically.

A complex kind of learning is required to become able to manage this demanding role competently. There is a great deal to be gained from understanding theory and having supervised clinical experience in order to learn technique: these two aspects of learning inform and grow out of each other, as reading this book should make clear. It is, of course, possible to read and re-read the classic authors in the field and learn new things at any time, particularly with growing experience of therapeutic work. However, in addition to all this, self-development is essential. The therapist's personal qualities, in particular her capacity to manage difficult emotions (both her own and the client's), to respond in a contained and thoughtful way and to remain available and responsive to the client's underlying needs, are absolutely crucial. Combining the elements of theory, practice and self-development involves an extensive personal learning process. In order to become competent therapists, rather than learning a technique we have to learn both a way of thinking and a way of being – what might be called a psychodynamic sensibility – something which goes on changing and hopefully deepening throughout our lives.

Conclusion

In providing this brief overview of the aims, patterns and experiences of change in psychodynamic therapy we have attempted, as far as possible, to avoid relying on specific theoretical conceptualisations of these processes. Psychodynamic theory is complex and multifaceted – its basic ideas will be introduced in Chapter 2. It would be idle to pretend that the theoretical and technical models which a therapist favours do not influence the character and development of the therapeutic process, although perhaps not as much as the personality of the therapist herself. Each theoretical model, indeed each facet of that model, proposes a vision of what beneficial change might be and how it might be achieved. In Part II we offer one way to conceptualise these change processes within a framework that offers a degree of cohesion in this multifarious literature. The question of how change occurs will be approached from a variety of angles within this section and then reviewed again from a broader perspective in Part III.

Note

1. We have opted to use the feminine pronoun in generic references to the therapist and client. This is intended to be inclusive of both genders.

There is no single psychodynamic theory – of change or of anything else. Instead we are faced with a tradition of developing ideas: a broad river, with various channels and cross-currents, which follows a shifting course with uncertain boundaries that change over time. Freud anticipated this prospect and he didn't like it! He wished to define and protect the core of his ideas from what he saw as adulteration: he tried to 'canalise' the river – but he failed. In the arena of understanding human development and facilitating it, competing visions, differing assumptions and a wide variety of possible conceptualisations have led to a never-ending debate; sometimes it seems almost a circus. While alternative traditions have emerged – particularly the humanistic, the cognitive-behavioural and the systemic, each with its own disputes and divisions – psychoanalysis is the rootstock of all psychotherapy. As a consequence, it has reproduced within itself many of the debates of the entire field and contains a multiplicity of ideas and approaches. The term psychodynamic is now used generically to encompass the diversity of theoretical approaches that remain connected to these psychoanalytic roots.

What does psychodynamic mean?

Within the array of ideas and approaches that constitutes the psychodynamic tradition, there does exist a unity of outlook which holds the different strands together. This is not the enforced unity of ideas that Freud once thought was essential to protect the analytic ideal from watered-down versions or wild practitioners. Nevertheless, certain key perspectives and perhaps some shared values constitute the core of a coherent approach. At its most basic, what is shared exists at the level of the perception of the human condition rather than its conceptualisation: it is, in a sense, pre-theoretical. This shared vision forms the basis of a recognisable clinical orientation – a sensibility about the nature of therapeutic practice – rather than a coherent psychological paradigm. At its best, this commonality of approach enables constructive dialogue and mutual learning within the tradition with the constant differentiation and subsequent reintegration of diverse ideas.

What ideas constitute the core of the psychodynamic approach? Perhaps the most fundamental idea is the focus on psychological or emotional pain – often thought of as anxiety and conceptualised in terms of internal conflict – but most fundamentally, simply pain. Life is thought of as a difficult and demanding process and the psyche is built and continues to develop in the struggle to deal with it. What is 'dynamic' is the turbulence created in the currents of mental life by these struggles. Means of avoiding pain are created: ways of seeing, thinking, feeling and behaving can all serve this purpose. These are the 'mechanisms' of defence. Much of this activity takes place out of awareness. There is, as it were, an 'internal' world different from external reality, the unconscious elements of which have a fundamental influence on the conduct of life. These unconscious attempts to avoid pain often fail: they are ineffective, unhelpful or self-limiting. This failure to manage unbearable pain gives rise to 'psychopathology'. Our failing defences are what give form to and maintain patterns of psychological disorder. They thus contribute to our difficulties in living, at least those that psychotherapy might properly help with.

This view of human life, personal development and psychological functioning underpins the 'clinical theory' of psychodynamics. This is the common sub-stratum of ideas that inform and guide the therapist's thinking and actions in the 'real world' of working with an individual client (Wallerstein, 1988). At this theoretical level, it is possible to pull together (to some extent at least) the competing psychodynamic conceptualisations of psychological development and structure. This book pursues this integrative trend of finding commonalities between different approaches. It emphasises these but points to key areas of disagreement and debate when these have implications for therapeutic technique and the handling of the clinical session.

Freud, in his most encompassing definition of psychoanalysis, suggested that it was in essence the study of the processes of resistance and transference (Freud, 1914). These ideas are at the heart of the clinical theory, defining psychodynamics in terms of the *process* of therapeutic change. Resistance is the tendency of people to defend themselves against the demands of therapy and the threat of a change in awareness. Transference is the manifestation of unconscious conflicts rooted in early development repeated in the therapeutic relationship. Psychodynamic therapy at its heart is about getting in touch with thoughts and feelings which were previously 'warded off', kept hidden from the conscious mind because they seemed to be too much to deal with. In overcoming or dissolving resistance, the aim is to increase a person's capacity to see themselves and the world for what they are and to tolerate the discomfort that this might involve. The vehicle for this is the relationship with the therapist, whose task and developed capacity is to face uncomfortable truths. The therapeutic relationship does not merely support the client in increasing awareness, but is the source of vital information about the painful experiences that lie at the root of the client's defensive distortions. It does this through the transferential process of recreating the old conflicts in the new setting of therapy. The understanding that the therapist develops with the client expands the client's awareness of these conflicts and opens up new options for managing them. The client's capacity to bear emotional pain and cope constructively with dissatisfaction is enhanced and the ability to reflect on experience and be curious about it is developed. These improved psychological abilities should allow for life experience to be used in the service of further development after therapy has finished.

Models of the mind

This brief summary of the psychodynamic outlook, emphasising what is common among different writers and simplifying the concepts to their most basic elements, greatly underplays the complexity and intricacy, indeed the sheer quantity, of psychodynamic theory. It also glosses over the way in which the debates and theoretical differences have become organised historically into opposing schools and the degree of passion with which rival positions are held. Inspired by Freud's own fascination with theoretical precision and by the fertility of his mind, the basic ideas have been subject to elaboration to a degree that is unparalleled among other approaches to psychotherapy. Freud's theoretical energy meant that his own ideas continued to develop and change over the course of his life. Not only is there no single psychodynamic model, there is no unitary Freudian one either. The psychodynamic approach can therefore be frustratingly difficult to grasp and establish coherently in one's mind. This is partly because it is dealing with areas that are intrinsically slippery and obscure, but it is also because some of its concepts have changed meaning over time and can be used in more than one way.

This development of Freud's model of the mind is sometimes articulated in terms of three historical periods. These are outlined in Box 2.1. However, even this outline simplifies things considerably. In a sense, each of these periods and their associated models remain alive within subsequent theorising, much as the earlier phases of development do in the current life of a person. In spite of Freud's wish to arrive at a comprehensive integrated theory, inconsistencies abound. This is partly because the changing emphases of his evolving theories originated from attempts to address different clinical issues and questions.

Box 2.1 Freud's Developing Theory

Affect/Trauma Theory 1890–1900

In collaboration with Breuer, Freud developed a theoretical understanding of hysterical symptoms (see also Box 3.1). Their core idea was of dissociation, a defensive process in which some experiences were split off from consciousness. The dissociated experiences were the affects associated with traumatic events, such as sexual abuse. To uncover the memory of these events, Freud used various adaptations of hypnotic technique, but over time he abandoned this in favour of employing 'free association'. In 1897 Freud significantly revised these theories, laying the stress on the internal roots of conflict associated with the distortion of external events by unconscious fantasy. This laid the foundation for psychoanalysis proper in his seminal book *The Interpretation of Dreams* published in 1900.

Topographical Theory 1900–20

Collecting a small band of followers, Freud elaborated the main tenets of psychoanalytic theory. Fundamental was the idea of a dynamic unconscious operating in a different way from ordinary consciousness. Unconscious fantasy driven by wish fulfilment was at the core of mental life. There was a strong emphasis on instinctual drives and the constant tension between the pleasure derived from their discharge and the restrictions of reality. The defining events that shape character took place in the first five years of childhood and – shockingly for the times – these were associated with the development of the child's sexuality. As these ideas were extended and attracted widening interest, psychoanalysis became a 'movement'. Disputes within it were often bitter and became the cause for expulsions.

The Structural Theory 1920–40

Recognising the importance of personal relationships in development, Freud introduced the idea of the internalisation of these as a means of coping with loss. This was the foundation for the later evolution of 'object relations' theories. It also moved interest towards understanding the mental structures that deal with instinctual conflicts. Freud's structural theory proposed a notion of three mental 'agencies', the id, the ego and the superego, existing in an equilibrium that governed mental life.

Anxiety is seen as a signal of internal threat to that equilibrium. Drive theory was also changed, highlighting the place of aggression in psychological functioning and introducing the idea of the 'death instinct', which has always been controversial. By Freud's death in 1939, there was a huge expansion of interest in psychoanalysis internationally. This set the scene for increasing theoretical differentiation in the years that followed.

Perhaps the best way to begin to grasp the theoretical range of the psychodynamic approach is to recognise that it contains a number of complementary 'points of view' rather than any one agreed model (Rappaport, 1959). Here we will emphasise three points of view that run through psychodynamic thinking about psychological functioning and change: the *dynamic*, the *structural* and the *developmental*. The dynamic point of view is, as the name suggests, the core perspective that we have already begun to examine – that of emotional conflict as underlying and motivating how we relate to the world. The structural point of view is the one emphasised in the outline of Freud's theoretical development in Box 2.1: it views functioning in terms of the framework of mental mechanisms which control it (for example, the tripartite 'structural theory'). The developmental point of view emphasises the roots of present psychological life as lying in the past and evolving over time through an individual's life span. It also conceptualises the adult as still motivated by an infantile mental life operating in the present. Although the outline of Freud's changing ideas is presented in structural terms in Box 2.1, changes in the other points of view were taking place in parallel. Elaborations and reconfigurations of each of these perspectives continued in the decades following his death. We shall return to outline the changes in this growing field and the debates they engendered later in this chapter. First, we shall elaborate the fundamental psychodynamic concepts from each point of view.

The dynamic point of view

The dynamic perspective sees mental life as a shifting flow constantly influenced by interacting forces. Fundamentally, as articulated in Freud's earliest theorising, these forces concern psychic pain and the wish to avoid it. Pain was initially thought of as the product of trauma, a consequence of externally imposed hurts, the memory of distressing events. A crucial move was made in seeing the source of pain as more fundamental, as having inevitable internal roots: pain is identified as being due to internal conflict between parts of the self. The nature of these conflicting internal

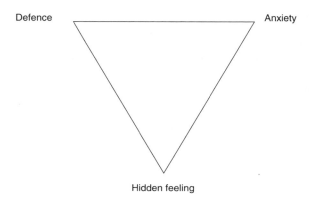

Defence   Anxiety

Hidden feeling

Figure 2.1 The triangle of conflict

forces can be conceptualised in various ways. Freud thought in terms of a pleasure principle – a drive for immediate gratification of instinctual impulses – opposed by a reality principle which delayed the expression of these wishes in the interests of adaptation to the constraints imposed by the external world, both social and physical.

The social pressures on the expression of desire might lead us to think of the conflict in terms of acceptable and unacceptable aspects of the self. Perhaps the most useful and flexible way of conceptualising this is shown diagrammatically in Figure 2.1 in what is commonly known as the 'triangle of conflict' (Malan, 1979). This portrays conflict as arising from a 'hidden feeling', which can be a wish or an impulse. However, this arouses anxiety. Freud later called this signal anxiety because it is a response to an internal threat, something that might disturb or threaten the individual's equilibrium. The reason for this disturbance is that the expression of the hidden feeling is in conflict with another perceived need so that it is feared to have catastrophic consequences. Thus a feeling of anger or rage and an associated impulse to hurt is disturbing, perhaps unacceptable, in the context of a relationship in which you are dependent on the other person and so need their love or good opinion or continued well-being. Expressed as thoughts, the conflict becomes: 'I hate you' *but* 'I am afraid that I will destroy our relationship which I need'. As Freud's later theorising came to see it, there are broadly speaking two general types of conflict: the fear of losing control and being overwhelmed by one's impulses; and the fear of transgressing internalised social standards and of being punished for it.

The anxiety signals that there is an internal danger situation. Some action must be taken to avert the threat posed by the conflictual aspects of the self or ambivalent state of mind. The 'solution' is to avoid conscious acknowledgement of the conflict. This is the third element in the triangle – the process of defence. Where the person does not have the capacity to tolerate or cope consciously with the threat posed by an internal conflict, some aspects must be warded off. Without this alteration in the nature of experience, the continuation of an unmanageable conflict becomes a threat to personal coherence: there is a feeling that the personality would disintegrate; it cannot hold together in the face of the conflict.

This defensive alteration of experience is a kind of self-deception. Some aspect of the self is disguised and there are a myriad of ways in which this can be achieved. An initial cataloguing of the many 'mechanisms' used to defend the integrity of the personality in the face of conflict was attempted by Freud's daughter, Anna Freud (1936). Such lists can help to alert us to the recurrent ploys and devices that people use but they may be unhelpful in suggesting an overly mechanical view of the process. Almost any element of experience can be used defensively in some context or other. It is, however, helpful to have a sense of how serious the alteration made to the experience of reality is. Thus it is usual to think of more or less 'healthy' kinds of defence. *Repression*, which involves keeping some impulse or emotion out of conscious awareness, is a relatively straightforward form of avoidance. It involves only the distortion of one element of our internal reality, although it often lays the foundation for further defensive transformations of it. *Dissociation* involves cutting off a whole area of self-experience with an associated complex of feelings, memories and aspects of the self: the alteration to internal reality is more far-reaching. *Denial* can be thought of as more severe again, involving the disavowal and distortion of significant aspects of both internal and external reality. Defensive processes may also be relatively specific to one situation or a rather generalised strategy that a person employs to distort much of their experience. Certainly, however, we all have our ways of defending ourselves; to the extent that these are routinely employed they are built into our very character structure. Thus the styles with which we typically relate to the world – careful and controlled, dramatic and colourful, fearful and withdrawing, and so on – can be seen as essentially complicated assemblages of our preferred defensive manoeuvres.

A number of consequences follow from this tendency to distort awareness to sustain a sense of internal coherence. It means that crucial elements of our actions are rendered out of conscious control. As a result we are poorly equipped to manage our true internal state and less able to adapt our behaviour to the external world. We are less able to anticipate damaging consequences of our actions or to learn from our experience. We may blindly repeat patterns of behaviour again and again. When routine defences don't work well enough to fully manage a conflict, further measures have to be resorted to as a second line of defence. Often these take the form of a 'symptom'. This is understood as a solution to a conflict through the formation of a compromise in which both sides of the conflict find a way of being expressed. Both the need to keep a wish out of awareness and the force of the wish itself can be felt in these situations. For example, obsessional checking is often thought to be a way of managing unacceptable hostility: the feared damage which results in imagination from the hostility requires the constant reassurance of the checking; meanwhile the hostility presses for expression in the compulsive quality of the behaviour and achieves some of its effect by torturing the person, and those round them, with its frustrating repetitiveness. Such manifestation of the underlying impulse in a distorted form has been called 'the return of the repressed'.

From the dynamic point of view, psychopathology is understood as the unmanageable anxiety generated by internal conflicts and the rigidities and restrictions in behaviour and experience created by compulsive defences. The aim of therapy is to reduce the hold of the defences, to facilitate greater flexibility and thus to increase the scope for choice. Change is seen as the resolution of conflict and integration of parts of the personality that have been defended against, leading to a wider ownership of all aspects of the self. Such change has to overcome the active resistance to a more inclusive awareness arising from the person's defensive system.

The structural point of view

The structural perspective focuses on the model of the mind, the overall framework within which psychological functioning is understood. In psychodynamic theory the principle feature of this psychological map is the presence of the unconscious. This is the core insight, Freud's greatest innovation. The notion of the mind as identical with conscious awareness is discarded. Freud believed this to be a revolutionary change of perspective: our relationship to our self is fundamentally altered; we are no longer 'masters in our own house'. There is a certain mysterious, even paradoxical, quality to the very idea of the unconscious and although it is now accepted as a commonplace in everyday thinking, there has been considerable debate about how it can be understood and what its implications are. Freud was by no means the sole originator of the concept of the unconscious (Ellenberger, 1970). His achievement was to use the idea in a detailed way to expand our understanding of day-to-day human functioning. He contrasted the way in which the conscious realm functioned with that of the unconscious and proposed that although the unconscious seems to be chaotic and incomprehensible, in fact its functioning is patterned; it has a logic of its own.

The key idea is that there are two different forms of mental life – different levels of organisation operating according to different rules – which Freud called primary and secondary process. The secondary process is mental life 'as we know it'. It is the realm of verbal syntax and logic, of abstract conceptualisation and clear delineation of difference: well-defined objects relate to each other in time and space in predictable ways. The world of primary process is quite different. Within it relationships are unconstrained by the laws of normal logic: there are no opposites and no negation so that contradictory propositions co-exist without challenge; there are no ordered sequences and so no sense of time; there is no clear division between different things or between subject and object, thus one thing can stand for another (displacement) or for many things at once (condensation); meanings are absolute rather than conditional and there is no doubt or degrees of certainty. Primary process may thus be thought of as the realm of internal rather than external reality; here the pleasure principle operates, insisting on the immediate gratification of impulse; everything is at once single-minded and fluid. The logic of primary process means that mental phenomena in the realm of the unconscious take on qualities of strangeness and uncanniness – they can be thought of as having a similar character to dreams.

One radical implication of Freud's vision of the unconscious is that all behaviour is purposeful and motivated. This is generally thought of in terms of the principle of 'psychic determinism': we can look for the psycho-logical causes of every thought and action by seeking its unconscious roots. Expanding this implication in a less mechanistic way, we might say that a fundamental principle of psychodynamic thinking is that all human activity is meaningful: it has potential significance. This is as much an ethos, a statement of intention, even of faith, as it is a scientific or psycho-logical model. It defines what psychodynamic therapists are trying to do. Freud demonstrated this approach dramatically in a series of early works in which obscure or seemingly meaningless areas of activity were inter-preted in terms of the principle of psychodynamic functioning and the logic of the unconscious. He thus opened up new areas of meaning in respect of dreams, everyday accidents and slips of the tongue, humour and myth as well as psychological symptoms. These were not to be thought of as signs of disorganisation or omission or chance, but as posi-tive creations, understandable in dynamic terms. They were not confined to the mentally ill, but something which all of us are subject to all of the time.

Freud was able, in this way, to use the model of the unconscious as a frame for interpreting the presence of hidden meaning. Its manifestations are never direct but always transformed and disguised by the need to maintain repression. The unconscious expresses itself, but what we see is the 'manifest' content. The 'latent' meaning can only be unravelled through a careful process of detective work. This involves interpreting the signs through knowledge of the way that unconscious transfor-mations work, to arrive at the unconscious wishes that lie at their source. The idea of the dynamic unconscious enabled later psychodynamic ther-apists to think in terms of an internal world, peopled by fantasy-laden figures in relationship with each other and operating according to the laws of primary process. This internal world is thought of as existing in constant interplay with external reality. The two may fit more or less well together but it is the internal world that is felt to be the dominant force structuring our perception of reality. By selection and manipulation, all situations, especially people and relationships, can be made to conform to its assumptions and expectations.

The relationship between the two forms of mental functioning (and their association with the dynamics of mental conflict) were initially articulated in what Freud termed the topographic model of the mind. This proposed the existence of three 'systems' of consciousness. Between the conscious and the unconscious systems sits the preconscious, ideas which one could be aware of but are not the focus of conscious attention at the moment. In fact, this idea points to a more elaborate vision of the relationship between consciousness and unconsciousness, one in which there is a series of levels of awareness and potential awareness. For example, there is an important difference between the repressed unconscious – disturbing thoughts and feelings arising from dynamic conflict which are defended against and excluded from awareness – and the deep unconscious – material which has never entered conscious awareness and that perhaps never could, in principle, be part of consciousness (see Chapter 8). This more flexible view of the operation of the unconscious is closer to some of the models that have recently emerged in cognitive psychology (Power and Brewin, 1991).

Freud struggled with a related issue concerning the operation of the mechanisms of defence within the topographic model. Where did these repressive forces, which excluded conflictual material from consciousness, sit in the system? If they were in the preconscious but *knew* the unconscious ideas that they excluded from consciousness, it would follow that the excluded material was not really unconscious at all. There was thus a paradox about the idea of defence. It suggested to Freud that even more of mental life is unconscious than implied by the topographical model and he proposed a substantial new model of the mind to explain this. This was the famous tripartite division into three mental agencies: the id, the ego and the superego (see Figure 2.2). This model is generally known as the 'structural theory'. The id is the repository of the drives, the fundamental motivating forces of mental life, which operate according to the primary process. They are never able to be conscious in themselves, but only become manifest as 'derivatives'. The superego is the internalised restraints of the social world as transmitted through the parents. Between these forces the ego mediates, balancing social and instinctual demands with the pressures and constraints of reality in an endeavour to maintain a psychological equilibrium. Crucially in this model, substantial elements of both the ego and the superego lie outside awareness in the unconscious system. What Freud originally called the 'censor', the function that screens consciousness from the disturbing effects of unacceptable wishes (in other words the operation of defensive processes) has to take place outside the realm of consciousness itself in order to be effective. The contents thus excluded from consciousness are pushed into the id, depleting and distorting the ego in the process.

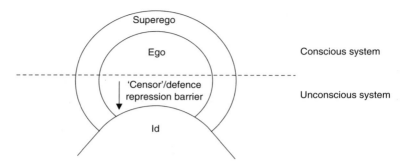

Figure 2.2   The structural model of mind

Importantly, Freud's original vision is somewhat less mechanistic than this picture implies. He did not use the impersonal Latin forms id and ego, but the ordinary German for 'it' and 'I' (Bettlelheim, 1983). He was conceptualising our relationship with ourselves in terms of a part with which we identify and seems personal and human – our subjectivity – and a more alien, impersonal aspect of ourselves, one which challenges our sense of personhood. In fact, a less 'structural' view can be taken of the idea of the unconscious generally. The word can be used more as an adjective than a noun. This suggests less a vision of a mysterious realm and more the process of restricting or expanding awareness and of discovering meaning. The unconscious in this view stands as the locus of potential meaning; it emphasises the possibility of areas of action that were out of conscious control coming within the scope of our influence. We become more meaningful to ourselves and in doing so gain a wider ownership of our lives. Things that formerly just happened can now be understood in terms of our complex and conflicting personal wishes.

In the structural point of view the aim of therapy is to make conscious what was unconscious, or as Freud's (1933) later theory formulated it: 'where "It" was, there "I" shall be'. Psychopathology is figured as a loss of freedom; it consists of actions arising from a lack of awareness and so lack of control. Change is thus seen in terms of an increased capacity to take responsibility for our behaviour and to widen ownership of ourselves through an expansion of awareness and meaning. The 'structural theory' is clear too about the limits to change: we are always engaged in a balancing act caught between conflicting demands. However, if the ego is strengthened and the power of the primitive superego reduced, a more effective, satisfying and less self-defeating balance is achievable.

The developmental point of view

In the developmental point of view we look to the past to understand the present. While this has in some ways become a commonplace of

Table 2.1   Phases of development

Age	Freud's classical libido theory	Erikson's 'psychosocial' stages/issues
0–1	Oral	Trust v. Mistrust
1–3	Anal	Autonomy v. Shame/doubt
3–5	Phallic/Oedipal	Initiative v. Guilt
6–puberty	Latency	Industry v. Inferiority
Adolescence	Puberty (drive resurgence)	Identity v. Identity diffusion
Early adulthood	Genitality	Intimacy v. Isolation
Middle adulthood		Generativity v. Self-absorption
Late adulthood		Integrity v. Despair

psychology – childhood as being both different from and crucially influential on adulthood – this perspective originated in and remains strongly associated with psychodynamic theory. Early life is considered of fundamental significance. It is formative of those aspects of mental life (including the dynamic and the structural) that are of central concern for understanding present dysfunction and future change. Unlike later developmental psychology, it was largely from adult accounts of that dysfunction in therapy and of memories of childhood experiences that the picture of the early years was built up. This picture in turn became a lens through which the struggles of adulthood were viewed.

Perhaps the main element of this psychodynamic construction of childhood is the idea of a sequence of developmental phases through which the growing child passes. Practically every new psychodynamic model grounds itself in a revised version of such a developmental scheme. Freud's original theory was famously (and contentiously) framed in terms of the evolution of childhood sexuality, especially in the first five years of life. This picture was conceptually underpinned by a theory of motivation rooted in instinctual energies of which libido – the drive for erotic pleasure – was prime. The developmental model was organised in terms of the bodily zones through which libidinal energies were experienced and expressed at different phases of childhood. However, these erogenous zones – the oral, anal and phallic – also characterised particular modes of relationship with caretakers that seem to have a much wider significance than just deriving pleasure. For example, the idea of an oral phase highlights issues of taking in sustenance, of dependency on others for life and also issues of what is inside and what outside, of who is who. Erikson (1950) later portrayed these libidinal phases in terms of a sequence of psychosocial issues that highlighted this relational dimension of the developmental sequence (see Table 2.1). In addition, Erikson – following Jung's lead on this issue – extended the process and sequence of development throughout adult life.

Whether one thinks of this theory of childhood sexuality as a vital pointer to the way in which early life is grounded in bodily experience, or whether it is viewed principally as a metaphorical insight into the forms of early interpersonal relatedness, is a matter of theoretical preference. It should not obscure how this developmental sequence has provided a foundation for numerous subsequent creative efforts to characterise the child's earliest ways of experiencing the world. Freud's view was of a series of elements or part-instincts, which became integrated in successful development leading to their mature expression in the genital phase. Subsequent theories emphasising interpersonal attachments have organised the course of development in a similar way; for example, as a narrative of progressive separation and differentiation from an early unity towards individuation and integration into a coherent sense of identity (Mahler et al., 1975).

Whatever the scheme, a key idea of the developmental point of view is that subsequent dysfunction is closely associated with problems occurring at particular developmental stages. Childhood difficulties – whether thought of as stemming from the quality of environment and care giving, the occurrence of problematic life events or from sources more internal to the child's changing instinctual and mental life – can block the developmental process, hindering or distorting further progress. Associated with this idea is the further notion that the seriousness of dysfunction depends on how early the developmental disruption occurred and how severe it was. Thus problems in the first year of life – Freud's 'oral stage' – such as a deficit in caretaking due to a mother being incapacitated by depression or absent through illness, could cause fundamental developmental damage, resulting in distortions to the basic sense of reality and whether the world and people in it can be experienced as dependable. This focus on the earliest years of life has often met with scepticism, even derision. However, psychodynamic theory has been proved right in many respects. As the study of the real infant (rather than the therapeutically reconstructed one) has grown, understanding of the formative role of events and relationships at this time has deepened (for example, see Stern, 1985).

This linkage between the original timing of developmental problems and both the nature and severity of their consequences is due to a central feature of the psychodynamic developmental point of view. Unlike developmental psychology in general, psychodynamic theory interprets the present directly in terms of the developmental past: the past is 'alive' in the here and now. Dysfunction is to be thought of as repetition. Patterns of feeling, thinking and acting which were established in previous developmental contexts are replayed in current, often very different, situations. These patterns are rigid and not readily open to correction through new experience. Indeed, present experience comes to be actively organised in terms of patterns that were current at some earlier time. Thus infantile modes of experience and behaviour persist but in a way that is sealed off from the influence of the present day. A person is to be understood as containing a baby or young child alive within them who shapes aspects of experience on the model of the past. Early patterns of relating to the world, normal at their appropriate developmental phase, are then a template for understanding the nature of current psychological dysfunction.

Psychodynamic theory has often been accused of focusing on the past to the exclusion of the present and future and of seeing a person's history as totally determining their current behaviour. This is not entirely fair. The developmental point of view looks to the past in order to cast light on what might be thought of as the personal context in which certain existential 'decisions' were originally made. Such decisions persist through being repeated and then ramify in their consequences. Repetitive patterns, thus established, often create self-perpetuating cycles. Complex lines of development are set in motion and character is formed cumulatively and interactively. In this sense, individuals are seen as both the product and the creator of their life history.

Framing understanding in the light of development enables people to acknowledge less acceptable aspects of their personality. The developmental point of view sees psychopathology as a kind of immaturity – the dominance of, or regression to, infantile modes of experience. The problem is thus a form of stuckness, a failure to develop. The aim of therapy is variously defined as some ideal of development: the genital character; the individuated person and so on. Generally the direction of maturation is thought of in terms of a greater integration of partial or fragmented components of the personality persisting from childhood. The process of change is through facilitating development, freeing up the blocked processes and enabling the normal course of maturation and integration to be re-started.

Disputed theoretical territory

The dynamic, structural and developmental points of view are central to the psychodynamic outlook and help to unite its different traditions. Within this common ground, however, many variants have arisen. Specific models have been proposed which articulate key features of these points of view, some drawing out and elaborating aspects of the earlier theories, some radically revising central tenets of them. Psychodynamic theory has changed and developed both during Freud's lifetime and subsequently. This is a sign of the liveliness and fertility of an intellectual discipline underpinned and informed by the demands of therapeutic practice. Psychodynamic theory may be awarded full marks for creativity. However, it gets little credit for the way in which this outpouring of ideas has sometimes been managed. Splits and schisms have characterised the psychodynamic arena. Bitter feuds, denunciations, excommunications and pressure to toe the line have been prevalent. This has restricted dialogue and stifled critical debate. It is a culture that has persisted until relatively recent years.

The process of proliferation and dispute started early. Within a decade of Freud's gathering of a group to work with him in developing his psychoanalytic project, some – unsurprisingly – started to take divergent paths. This process continued over the following years with some of the disagreements being contained within the institutions of the psychoanalytic movement while others led to splits and departures. Along with many lesser figures, some of these 'heretics' were great thinkers in their own right and the 'schools' that they founded have flourished separately within the broader psychodynamic field. At the same time, the developing course of psychoanalytic theory itself produced a number of theoretical models and therapeutic techniques that differed significantly from each other. Some of the main figures and positions as they originated and exist today are outlined schematically in Figure 2.3.

How is it that these creative developments have taken on the divisive character that they did? Freud himself had a very creative mind but quite an ambitious and controlling personality. In a sense, he set the trend of 'brand naming' schools of therapy, each with a charismatic founder. A feature of the subsequent developments within psychoanalysis has been the need to return to Freud to seek legitimation in his writing for subsequent changes and additions. This is not difficult since the ambiguities and contradictions of his theories provide fertile ground either for confusion or for stimulating further developments. In a sense, the psychodynamic tradition is the initiator of all subsequent psychotherapeutic practice in all its bewildering diversity. It is hardly surprising that there is scope for differences concerning all the fundamental issues of therapeutic practice to be articulated and played out within psychodynamic theory itself as it has evolved over the period of a century. Perhaps most fundamentally, the power of what is at issue and the emotional demands of therapeutic practice are bound to affect the way in which the ideas themselves evolve. Psychodynamics deals with human passion. It should be no surprise that it becomes itself passionate, often in ways that are hard to manage maturely.

Since the 1980s there has been a growing acceptance of the legitimacy of the diverse positions within the psychodynamic arena. The tendency to either overemphasise or downplay differences has been lessened. There has been increasing acceptance of a situation of pluralism in which a number of major positions exist, each with its own traditions and key theoretical contributions. Perhaps these are not amenable to any easy resolution, but this acceptance of difference allows greater clarity about which differences are substantive and which are more a matter of appearance or language. The main lines of historical debate can now be viewed more dispassionately and placed in terms of their contribution to the present day. Broadly speaking, these disputes have existed with regard to two major issues in psychodynamic theory: the nature of motivation and the roots of psychopathology. The evolving positions on these issues provide

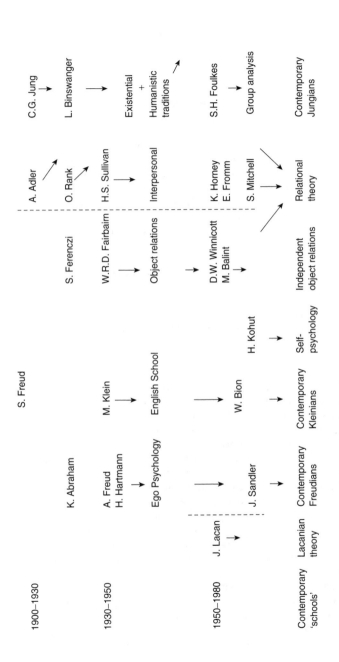

Figure 2.3 The developing theoretical field of psychodynamics

- - - - - Indicates the approximate institutional boundaries of the 'psychoanalytic movement'

a glimpse of the different models of human action that have been developed by some of the key contributors to psychodynamic thinking.

The nature of motivation

An important element of Freud's original vision was a model of motivation based on the operation of instinctual drives that underlay a person's relationship with the world. It was what has been called a 'hydraulic model': instinctual pressure builds up and is relieved through discharge. The relief of this tension was the aim of the drive whether this was sex or hunger or aggression. 'Objects', whether people or things, were required to fulfil this aim and patterns of behaviour and relationship were constructed through learning how to achieve this. The crucial drive in this process was, as reflected in the developmental theory, sexual. 'Libido' (the Latin for desire), however, was regarded in quite a broad sense; it covered a wide array of body-based relationships with the world. Later, partly in response to the criticisms of Adler, the place of aggression as a drive was elevated to an equal position and each of these concepts generalised to be encompassed in a polarity between 'life' and 'death' instincts. Although the language of instinct remained in place, it evolved in use from its original physiological emphasis.

In fact, questions about the nature of libido were being asked early on. They were a major source of the split with Jung, who abandoned the sexual, drive-based conceptualisation of libido for a more encompassing idea of creative energy reaching out for connection to the world. Jung (1934/1981) came to understand the form of that connection as structured through various transpersonal forms or 'archetypes' that were intrinsic to the human psyche in general. Although often not recognised as such, this broadening of the libido concept was the beginning of one of the major lines of development in psychodynamic thought: the nature of the relationship to the 'object' where this is a person. Starting in Freud's later writings and developed by Klein and others, a central place in understanding the structure and functioning of the psyche was given to the form in which relationships with people (particularly parental caregivers) were internalised to become the building blocks of inner reality. Initially conceived in terms of relationships produced through the functioning of the instinctual drives (hence the use of the term 'object') writers such as Fairbairn (1952) in Britain and Sullivan (1953) in America, proposed that there was instead an autonomous need for human relationship independent of the satisfaction of physiological needs. The human infant is seen as intrinsically 'object-seeking' and development is, more than anything else, the playing out of this need and the anxieties and difficulties associated with it: the self always evolves as part of a human relationship and the internal world is built out of this interplay.

A diverse group of 'object relations' theories arose from this understanding and came to dominate psychodynamic thinking by the last quarter of the twentieth century. Various thinkers (see Figure 2.3) elaborated different models, often endeavouring to reconcile this emerging view with Freud's original conceptualisation. It is, however, questionable whether these two contrasting models of motivation can be coherently integrated. Greenberg and Mitchell (1983) suggest that they are in fact two different paradigms, visions of motivation coherent in themselves but embodying different understandings of the human condition as a whole. Drive theory might be called a 'one-person psychology': it envisages a single biological organism in a struggle for self-preservation with its external environment, including other people; drives are essentially asocial. Object relations theory takes a fundamentally different view. It is a 'two-person psychology': the developmental context is always interpersonal from birth and the human personality, indeed the human mind, is fundamentally embedded in a social field – we not only seek objects, we are our objects.

Freud thought of his drive model of motivation as a crucial link to the biological basis of behaviour and so to a scientific underpinning of his theory as a whole. This was, of course, an understanding of science that was grounded in its historical time. Other biological and psychological foundations are now available to support the scientific credentials of an object relations point of view. Nevertheless, the appropriateness of even a broader vision of science as the best frame of reference for understanding psychodynamic theory has been seriously questioned. Various writers, particularly Lacan (1977) and others in the French tradition, suggested that the humanities offer a better epistemological basis for understanding the psychotherapeutic task. They propose a linguistic/interpretative or 'hermeneutic' understanding of what psychodynamic psychotherapists are up to: they are in the business of decoding texts, discovering and constructing meanings – they are not scientists. Arguably, this was always ambiguous in Freud's original, highly narrative writings: their scope always encompassed both perspectives. This ambiguity may even have functioned as a source of creative tension throughout the history of the psychodynamic movement (Ricoeur, 1970). However, there has always been some suspicion that the wish to abandon biology in psychodynamic theory hides a defensive desire to get away from the seamier side of human life. Grounding our understanding in bodily-based needs forces an appreciation that human beings are animals existing in an evolutionary context. As some see in Jung's writings, the move towards a general relational impulse can lead to a fascination with the abstract that removes us from the concrete and the personal. Similarly, object relations theories are sometimes accused of being too 'interpersonal' and so lacking appreciation of the inner world and its depths. Perhaps both can disguise the ordinariness, even the pettiness, of some of our fundamental motivations.

To be useful, psychodynamic theory needs to continue to challenge our tendency for self-idealisation while, at the same time, avoiding the pitfalls of reductionism.

The roots of psychopathology

The nature and sources of those developmental experiences that are thought of as being the source of later personal difficulty have been variously conceptualised. With these different views the nature of the dysfunction itself is altered and so too is its remedy, the kind of therapeutic change which is needed. In Freud's earliest model, pathogenic experience was thought to take the form of environmental trauma. Although difficulties were played out internally – in painful affects and the defences used to manage them – the root cause was external: specifically some form of abuse, often sexual. Controversially, Freud changed his views. Abandoning the 'seduction theory', he focused even more on sexuality but framed the difficulty in terms of internal conflict produced by the drive pressure of infantile libido, working largely in the realm of unconscious fantasy rather than real relationships.

Freud's critics have accused him of moral cowardice, of changing his mind and distorting his understanding of the truth in order to avoid confronting the scandal of widespread childhood sexual abuse (Masson, 1985). Perhaps. But Freud's views on infantile sexuality were hardly designed to win him popularity. Moreover, he did not deny the presence or influence of sexual experiences in childhood as his later case studies testify. His view was that it was the personal meaning of traumatic events and in particular their unconscious significance that crucially determined their impact in later life. This has remained a vitally important idea but it did focus attention away from the external environment towards an emphasis on the internal world. This had a significant effect on the scope of psychodynamic theory and practice over several decades and undoubtedly contributed to the widespread 'silence' about the abuse of children that has only recently been challenged.

The internal focus of the 'one-person' drive theory of motivation promoted a vision of psychopathology as something built into the human condition rather than as arising, principally, from adverse individual circumstances. In particular, the Oedipal situation of rivalry with one parent for the love of the other is thought of as representing a fundamental dilemma in human relationships: we are dependent on other people but are inevitably in conflict with them for the satisfaction of competing desires. Frustration, competition, fear and social restraint are built into our lives. Human beings are presented with dilemmas and conflicts that cannot be completely solved, only tolerated more or less well. It is these dilemmas that are the source of psychopathology. Where they cannot be managed effectively, symptoms take their place.

The place of aggression in the face of these dilemmas became increasingly important. In Freud's later theory, hostility always seemed to have a part to play in creating and perpetuating psychological dysfunction. However, a controversy that has run through psychodynamic theory concerns the nature and roots of aggression itself. Modelled on the drive theory of libido, Freud's notion of aggression is as a fundamental instinctual drive, autonomous and irreducible. In the forms of hatred, envy and spite this plays a central part in the Kleinian understanding of psychopathology: we are inevitably anxious because we are faced with an urge in ourselves to act destructively towards the things and people we depend on for life itself. However, a contrasting vision sees aggression as secondary to frustration of other needs by an environment that fails adequately to meet them. This view turns attention once again towards the outside world and perhaps specifically towards the quality of care giving. If circumstances are particularly frustrating, then a developing child will be enraged more frequently and aggression will play a correspondingly larger part in its mental life. This difference in view has had a significant impact on therapeutic technique and the importance that different schools attach to uncovering the client's hostility as opposed to focusing on her vulnerability and unsatisfied neediness. Conceptually, however, it is not clear that this theoretical dilemma is soluble or even real. Since frustration and dissatisfaction are inevitable features of human life (however good the care), a debate about aggression being primary or secondary does not take us very far. The theoretical polarisation around this point seems to have more to do with the therapeutic ethos and technical preferences of practitioners and, like all polarisations, may have displaced attention from the need to manage both sides of the issue.

As the debate on aggression demonstrates, the need for attention to the impact of environmental factors inevitably reasserts itself. For example, concerns about managing external reality were integral to the 'Ego Psychology' of Anna Freud (1936) and Hartmann (1958). In spite of this, these theorists remained relatively neglectful of the impact of external as compared to internal factors in understanding the developmental roots of dysfunction. A line of thinking stemming from the work of Ferenczi did exist, which placed more emphasis on the quality of care giving and its influence on future problems. Some object relations theories later highlighted the crucial role of the parental relationship, particularly that with the mother. Both Winnicott (1965) and Kohut (1977) suggested that an experience of 'good-enough' dependence provided by the mother's empathic attunement to the infant's needs and communications laid the foundation for future development. 'Deficits' in this were the source of psychopathology. The failure of the caretaking environment to provide what was needed for the child to flourish results in a lack of psychological structure at certain key points and creates gaps which have to be filled defensively with a 'false self' – an artificial persona and way of relating to others which conceals the internal lack arising from the unmet dependency needs.

These debates seem less pressing nowadays although they continue. The external and internal worlds are now thought of as existing in a dialectical interplay. The importance of the inner meaning of events and experiences, the conflicts they create and their elaboration in the personal world of the unconscious remain defining features of a psychodynamic approach. However, the context of internal and external events, including the subtle interplay within early care-taking relationships and the states of mind these involve, are regarded as forming the matrix out of which personality is created. Thus, early 'deficits' and 'traumas' are responded to by the child who manages them the best she can. These adaptations become the foundation for later distortions in relating which may maintain or exacerbate the early failures. None of these factors exists independently and all are played out over time.

The processes of change

In a sense, all theories, models and points of view embody metaphors for the human condition. They are ways of configuring a vision of psychological health and well-being and of its absence. They are also ways of focusing on aspects of change and how it might be promoted. Their influence is not only on how the therapist conceptualises her client's struggles and how she responds to them, but also on the way the client views herself, adding to or creating an alternative to the ways in which she already understands her suffering. Each of the models and the points of view outlined has been developed in the context of therapeutic work. They have been elaborated in order to serve the process of change and to support the therapist in what is a demanding role: they are more than just theorising. Above all, they can be thought of as 'listening perspectives': ways of hearing and understanding clinical material in a therapeutic session and hence as tools for empathy (Hedges, 1983).

We have emphasised the changing nature of theory in the psychodynamic tradition and of the diversity of models that have been developed within it. In spite of the commonalities present in the core sensibility and main points of view that define the psychodynamic approach, the field is faced for the time being with accepting a pluralistic situation – the existence of a number of well-developed competing approaches, each with its own models and assumptions. Nevertheless, as the psychodynamic tradition enters its second century, there have also been signs of convergence and the beginnings of integration among these different approaches (Wallerstein, 2002). In particular, the pervasive reciprocal influence of human beings on each other at an unconscious level – whether it is mother and infant, members of a family, lovers or enemies, team workers or therapist and client – is now understood to be central to human life. What we desire, the ways we subvert ourselves and the processes of personal growth and therapeutic change are all seen as crucially dependent on this interplay. In the subsequent chapters of this book we will assume the existence of this emerging convergence of perspectives while also drawing on the diversity of psychodynamic understandings to illuminate particular facets of the process of change. The authors' main training has been within the independent object relations tradition and the field of group analysis, and they have both been influenced by American relational approaches. Readers might wish to bear this in mind in developing their own listening perspective on the book.

The following six chapters deal with the processes of change as they have been conceptualised within the psychodynamic tradition. We offer a way of organising and thinking about these processes that encompasses a range of different, complementary, and sometimes competing, visions of how change takes place. This six-fold conceptualisation is only one way of organising this material, but it does have the advantage of enabling us (and the reader) to cover the many facets of the therapeutic process. The first three aspects – expression, understanding and relationship – explain the essential elements of the psychotherapeutic situation and technique and the main ways in which personal change has traditionally been thought to take place. The subsequent elements of the model – regression, differentiation and creation – address some deeper, more complex and debatable facets of change in the psychodynamic approach. These six facets, presented in this way, may look like a sequence, a map of the direction and course of change – an impression that could be emphasised by our use of a clinical example of the course of a single therapy running through these chapters. Although there is something in this, it would also be largely misleading. Each of these different facets of change is significant in its own right and is not dependent on taking its 'turn' in a linear process of progressive transformation. Such an overarching perspective on what is crucial in creating change – 'therapeutic action' in the jargon – is one we shall return to in the concluding chapter of the book.

Readers with little or no experience of psychodynamic psychotherapy might find it useful to read through the clinical example as a whole, to establish some sense of what a course of therapy can be like, before reading the individual chapters in Part II. We have constructed the example to give a flavour of a representative piece of work – not a perfect or in any way exceptional model. Nevertheless, it should be possible to view the content and processes depicted in each part of the example in the light of many of the ideas discussed in the associated chapter. We would encourage readers to construct and develop these links for themselves after they have read through the relevant theoretical material.

PART II
Processes of Change:
A Framework

When people seek therapeutic help they can be motivated by a variety of factors. One, however, is so common as to be almost ubiquitous: the desire to be free of something. It may be a disabling anxiety, a painful sense of isolation or a compulsive pattern of behaviour. Whatever the problem, the person feels caught up and trapped by it. With the mind in thrall to forces that appear only to perpetuate difficulties, all freedom of movement can seem to be lost – life feels stuck in a restrictive pattern. Some of Freud's early patients had quite literally lost their freedom of movement. They complained of physical paralysis or dysfunction that had no obvious organic cause. Their bodies were in the grip of something that Freud believed was really located in their minds. Psychoanalysis originated from his attempts to find a way of releasing such mental contents in order to free his patients from their disabling symptoms. Although psychodynamic theory has become more sophisticated, the aim of releasing the mind from neurotic restrictions has remained. To achieve this requires that we have some access to what is going on 'internally' – the mind must be expressed in some way.

Expression is a crucial foundation and vehicle for all other levels of therapeutic activity in psychodynamic practice; it provides the 'material' for the therapist to work with. In addition, the act of expressing thoughts and feelings – and hence of modifying awareness of them – does, in itself, seem to be one way in which change can occur. This is perhaps the most literal meaning of the 'talking cure': suffering may be transformed by speaking about it. The idea that we can obtain some relief from suffering by its expression is, of course, familiar in everyday language. We talk of 'getting it out of our system' or 'getting it off our chest', with the implicit idea that it can help to find a way to expel or re-position our problems in some way. The opposite of this is to remain 'burdened' by something, to 'keep things bottled up'. The images conjured by these phrases are of being forced to bear something without respite or being filled with something without any means of discharge. Either way we can end up feeling that we are 'cracking-up' under the strain or perhaps 'blocked' in what we can do. Expression carries the hope of achieving the relief we desire – but how and to what extent can it really deliver this?

Verbalisation, catharsis and confession

It is the emotional content of our experience that seems to most need and press for release. Emotions are closely connected with bodily states and can be expressed in physical action, both voluntary and involuntary. However, they can also be expressed more indirectly and symbolically in language. The development of psychotherapy as a talking cure has taken full advantage of this and has led to exploration of levels of emotional activity that would not otherwise readily become visible. This capacity of language to function as a therapeutic vehicle, rather than simply as a means of defence through intellectualising, has much to do with the complex dual quality that it possesses: it is linked to the dense undifferentiated mental states of the unconscious as well as to the discriminating conceptual activity of secondary consciousness. Language develops in our earliest years and retains its link to the emotional, relational and bodily processes that characterise this period of development (see Chapters 6 and 8). Psychodynamic psychotherapy has exploited these properties of the use of language and eschewed other means of fostering emotional expression such as those found in 'expressive' therapies based on art, drama and bodywork. While emotional expression is intrinsic to the psychodynamic approach, it has not remained as central as it is in these therapies, whose aim, derived from the cathartic model (see Box 3.1), is primarily to promote it.

The therapeutic significance of expression in psychodynamic therapy is, however, considerably more complex than is often recognised. For our purposes it is useful to distinguish three of the ways it can contribute to change. Most fundamentally this is via the process of verbalisation, which can lead to the more specific processes of catharsis and confession.

Verbalisation

Verbalisation is the process of expressing ideas and feelings in language – putting things into words. In the case of emotional difficulties this is a significant and far-reaching achievement and crucial to other processes of change in psychodynamic therapy. To express an emotional or other experience verbally requires an act of symbolisation: words have to represent or point to the experience and in doing so make it communicable. By giving verbal form to our experience we make it more visible to ourselves as well as to other people. We can then more easily reflect on it ourselves and benefit from the reflections of others. Indeed, we may not really know what we think until we try to say it and as we speak we may stimulate a further series of thoughts or feelings that otherwise would not have arisen. When mental and emotional life is given verbal form it is transformed into a symbolic order where further elaboration and change become possible. In this way verbalisation can be seen as an inherently transformative process: it puts experience into words and allows words to act on experience. What is unique in the psychodynamic approach, as we explain below, is the particular method that is suggested for the client's verbal expression within the therapeutic context.

Catharsis

The roots of the word 'catharsis' lie in the notions of purging and purification. Purging has the medical connotation of removing contaminants that cause illness while purification implies the more general quality of making clean. Aristotle applied the concept to the emotions in his analysis of the effects of the dramatic rendering of tragedy. He argued that the performance of tragedy aroused terror and pity in the audience and thus affected the release or discharge of these emotions. Anxieties were stimulated and feelings moderated through processes we would now describe as identification. This offered a beneficial and humanising experience for those who gave themselves up to it. Freud adopted the term to apply to his method of reviving and discharging emotional reactions arising from traumatic experiences that had been repressed from memory (Box 3.1). This 'abreactive' technique was based on the psychological model that intense emotions could lead to various forms of pathology unless they were discharged and that discharge required the full emotional experience of the traumatising event. Although far less central to modern conceptions of dynamic technique, writers such as Loewald (1980) and Laplanche and Pontalis (1973) point out that it remains an intrinsic feature of the analytic process. The basic aim of abreaction is to rid the system of troublesome emotions. Catharsis thus achieves change directly through the expression of emotion.

Box 3.1 The Cathartic Method

Freud and Breuer's collaboration culminated in the publication of *Studies on Hysteria* in 1895. They hypothesised that traumatic events lead to strong emotional reactions and that these, understood in terms of mental energy, are normally discharged through some form of action or direct expression. However, if the emotions are too intense or the circumstances do not allow for their immediate discharge, they could be diverted from their natural course and their precipitating events could be excluded from memory. The diverted emotions might then appear in a disguised or converted form, often in symptoms of a physical nature or in disabling anxieties about other things. Freud proposed that the emotional energy – unable to find proper discharge – could become 'strangulated' and that this led to these forms of pathology. The objective of treatment was thus to locate and discharge the underlying emotions directly. This was achieved by promoting recall of the traumatic experiences that were assumed to lie at their origin. The cathartic method was thus the therapeutic technique associated with the 'affect/trauma' theory introduced in Box 2.1.

The process of recall and release of emotion in this way is called 'abreaction' and can occur spontaneously or be triggered by external stimuli. The beneficial effect is assumed to arise as a result of the cathartic expression of the disturbing emotion. Originally Freud used hypnosis and direct suggestion to lead his patients to recall their forgotten experiences. In doing so he moved away from earlier attempts to remove symptoms directly to the attempt to remove what he assumed was their underlying emotional cause. This reflected a move away from the prevalent medical model towards a therapy grounded in psychological processes of change. In time he abandoned hypnosis completely, although the use of the couch in psychoanalysis remains, in some respects, a vestige of this. The emphasis on catharsis as the main effect of treatment has been superseded in psychodynamic theory. Nevertheless, it continues to be a potential element of therapeutic change.

Confession

To confess means to acknowledge or declare. It is a term we most commonly apply to the acknowledgement of fault or blame and thus has a much stronger moral connotation than the idea of catharsis. Confession requires a conscious acknowledgement of an act, thoughts or feelings rather than simply a discharge of emotion. It implies taking responsibility and making some open declaration of this. The effect of confession, unlike catharsis, is mediated by the real or imagined response of another person or figure to whom the confession is made – one who may carry the prerogative for punishment or forgiveness. At an emotional level personal confession is usually allied to disturbing feelings of guilt or shame. A declaration of fault or inadequacy releases these feelings from the private domain to an interpersonal one where the response received can either mitigate or intensify them. We may be forgiven or condemned. Here psychotherapy has sometimes been compared to the religious confessional: a place where guilt can be relieved and shameful shortcomings confronted so that life can be continued more freely. Confession may feel as if it clears or even purifies the mind and returns it to a state of greater integrity or equilibrium. As such it can be conceived as a restorative process. However, psychodynamic theory has undermined an uncritical acceptance of these benefits as it draws attention to the way confession typically involves a failure to own judgemental parts of the self – represented in the notion of the 'superego'. Instead it pursues relief through a reassuring identification of these aspects of the self with a figure of benign authority. It thus relies on maintaining the structure of this dependent relationship and may be used to avoid deeper psychological change. The psychodynamic approach seeks not to exploit the confessional elements of expression in therapy but to explore and question them in a search for more fundamental forms of change.

Both catharsis and confession usually rely on verbalisation to achieve their effects. However, verbal expression is a primary means of 'release' in its own right. Indeed, some writers, such as Bollas (1997), suggest that it has a fundamental priority in analytic work. The open expression and representation of thoughts and feelings may not necessarily lead to the same degree of immediate emotional relief promised by catharsis or confession, but beyond underpinning them both it provides a means of exploring and giving form to mental life. Psychoanalysis developed from an essentially purgative and restorative approach into a more deeply transformative one. To do so it had to discover a method that moved away from the prescriptive technique of hypnosis (see Box 3.1) towards a means of maximising the potential of verbal expression to give form to wider aspects of experience. This was achieved through a fundamental innovation: the method of free association.

Free association

Freud's original use of hypnosis relied on suggestion to lead the patient towards particular events or experiences. Gradually, under the influence of his self-analysis and the limitations he experienced with using hypnosis, he moved away from this approach towards a method that relied on the patient's own spontaneous expression. He encouraged patients to adopt a relaxed but attentive frame of mind and to simply voice whatever thoughts or ideas might occur to them. He described this approach as 'freier Einfall', which has been translated as free association. Perhaps more literally this means 'what falls into the mind' – there is no requirement to consciously associate or follow ideas, simply to report unreservedly whatever comes into awareness, however irrelevant, trivial, disagreeable, nonsensical or even inappropriate it may seem. This has come to be known as the 'fundamental rule' of the analytic situation. The intention is to speak spontaneously with a suspension of conscious control. In this process of free association, the client should also remain attentive to what she is disclosing, should in a sense be simultaneously a speaker and observer of her own thoughts. This process represents an unusual – even subversive – way of talking to oneself about oneself. It has been likened to a form of meditation.

Despite its apparent simplicity this is, in practice, a far from straightforward expectation. Most people find that there is considerable difficulty in allowing such an open communication of their thoughts and feelings to occur and find themselves consciously or unconsciously censoring what they report. However, the difficulties of freely associating are closely allied to its revolutionary significance as a tool for revealing not only the content of the mind but also the patterns of dynamic activity and constraint intrinsic to mental life. On a conscious level, this procedure can bring home just how much we ordinarily hesitate to say and so conceal. There are fears of being criticised by our therapist, of feeling foolish and ashamed, or of hurting her. Such conscious hesitations have been termed 'reluctance', as opposed to the less conscious retreats and self-protection of 'resistance' (Hartman, 1958). Free association can reveal, indirectly, secrets that we don't know we are harbouring. These are shown in gaps, hesitations or disjointed thoughts where something is excluded from consciousness as unbearable. The move to focusing on such signs of resistance as being important in their own right was crucial in the evolution of psychodynamic therapy – indeed, it was a major element in Freud's development of the free association method. Of course, the 'associations' are never truly 'free' but linked to (perhaps we might say, as Freud did, determined by) the network of unconscious ideas, wishes and fears that are active in the therapeutic relationship at the time. But there are relative degrees of 'freedom' involved – sometimes there is a greater experienced fluidity in which the client seems in fuller communication with herself and is willing to let the therapist in on this. As Bollas puts it: 'free association is always a "compromise formation" between psychic truths and the self's efforts to avoid the pain of such truths' (Bollas, 2002: 9). It has been suggested that, if anything, the capacity and willingness to free associate is an indicator of a positive outcome of therapy, rather than a necessary pre-condition.

The effect of the free association format is to open up the communication of aspects of mental life that are normally excluded from everyday conversation – unless revealed by accident, as in slips of the tongue, or in an indirect way such as humour. In effect it opens a route to unconscious as well as conscious processes. It is an arena in which we can experience ourselves in a new light, one that contrasts with our everyday self. It is a procedure for exploring the internal world, a means of getting 'news from within'. Behind this process is the idea that such contact with the unconscious comes only 'on its own terms'. What is needed is the fostering of a space for the spontaneous arrival of material – thoughts, memories, images, emotions, bodily feelings, day-dreams as well as the hesitations, gaps and slips in their recall – that derive from and are closer to the unconscious. As in dreaming, the constraints of reality and reason are temporarily put aside to allow for the novel and unexpected to arise and be expressed. This is a new type of listening to the self: being in touch with ourselves in this way Bollas (1987) calls 'evocation', a relaxed, non-vigilant state of mind, the creation of a receptive space. It forms the basis of a crucial form of self-experiencing, one that is prior to and provides a foundation for the kind of 'knowing' developed in the processes of interpretation and understanding (see Chapter 4). This requires a special kind of situation to be constructed in therapy, one that differs in many ways from the expectations of ordinary social encounters.

In normal practice, the fundamental rule is not applied rigidly. Rather it underpins the expectations and culture of psychodynamic work and characterises its exploratory nature. Its influence on the therapeutic interaction makes for an uncommon form of conversation. In briefer forms of therapy and counselling the significance of free association will be less obvious, but its trace remains in the quality of communication that is encouraged between the client and the therapist. The onus is very much on the client saying what is on her mind and allowing her thoughts to unfold in a way that is not determined by intrusive questioning or any predetermined agenda. In group analytic psychotherapy the equivalent process is described as a 'free floating discussion' (Foulkes, 1975). Again, no structure is imposed on the group but individuals are encouraged to openly contribute their thoughts and feelings as they arise in the group situation (see Chapter 9). In addition to this relatively free form of expression by the client, the therapist's 'listening perspective' is profoundly altered: whatever the client says will be heard in the light of it being a potential communication of something unconscious. What is expressed is not only taken literally.

The therapeutic situation

Along with the wish to be free of something, which people bring to therapy, there is also often the wish to be shown how. The therapist, after all, is a trained professional and has seen many people before, some of whom have presumably had similar problems. Like other professional experts they can be expected to offer an opinion, advice and hopefully a definite prescription as to what should be done. There may sometimes be an element of this in briefer forms of psychodynamic work but it is generally very circumscribed. The therapeutic approach seems to fly in the face of our expectations of being offered a solution. Indeed, the whole idea of free association turns normal, rational, goal-oriented thinking on its head: it is antithetical to 'problem-solving' or the focused pursuit of understanding; it subverts even the ordinary processes of communication and listening; it serves to break established and repetitive patterns of thought and expectation. What is being offered may at first be difficult to grasp, although its value in terms of releasing emotion and revealing unexpected connections is often quite quickly apparent. There are a several of features the therapist's attitude that contribute to this sense of the analytic situation being both unusual and yet potentially releasing.

Apparent passivity

In comparison with normal social expectations and indeed with many other forms of psychotherapy, the psychodynamic therapist seems relatively passive. She generally sits still and remains quiet, allowing the client to start wherever she wants and to talk about whatever she chooses. The rhythmic turn taking of everyday conversation is replaced by what can feel like an invitation to monologue. The opportunity exists for the client to fill the room with her own thoughts and feelings. There is no need to ask the therapist how she is, or to comment on the weather or the news, although the habit of so doing may at times be irresistible. Normal social conventions are gently lifted, but without the substitution of an alternative framework, apart from an invitation to 'voice whatever comes to mind'. There is no checklist of questions, just someone available to listen. The effect of this can be potent. For some it can be alarming and confusing. The therapist can appear withholding or even deliberately perverse. Strong feelings can quite quickly be provoked and expressed or a real difficulty can be encountered in putting thoughts and feelings into words at all. For others, however, the freedom to just talk and share burdensome experience can almost immediately feel quite liberating. The therapist's relative silence can give weight and seriousness to the client's words. It points up – as in a mirror – the ways those words might be used inauthentically and so subtly undermines our usual forms of concealment and dishonesty.

Even in supposedly direct, unmediated expression like free association there is always an implicit audience, an imagined listener to whom the self is speaking, even if this is only an internal one. Inevitably the therapist is placed in the role of the 'expected' listener: the issue of 'who' is being spoken to with what intention becomes crucial to the therapy through the analysis of the 'transference' relationship (see Chapter 5). However, it is as well to put paid at this point to the misleading idea (if taken too literally) that the therapist acts only as a 'blank screen'. This describes how material may be projected on to the therapist by the client but is not intended as a model of how the therapist should necessarily behave at all times even in more classical 'analytic' work. She is likely to need to be more active with some clients than others and at some points in therapy in contrast to others. Caution over self-disclosure and responding directly to questions is designed to keep the focus on the client's expressions and ultimately their meanings. It is not necessary to be socially insensitive or completely impersonal.

Attentiveness

The relative passivity of the therapist is accompanied by a quality of attentiveness that can have a profound influence on the atmosphere established in the room and ultimately on the nature of the client's own awareness. Simple attention can be cultivated and reflected through non-verbal means as well as the usual range of listening and responding techniques commonly taught as 'counselling skills' – albeit used in moderation. However, these techniques can become mechanical – they leave out of consideration the therapist's own state of mind. A state of openness and receptiveness to the client as well as to the totality of one's own internal responses and reactions is a key aspect of the psychodynamic method. This requires a quality of attentiveness that is open-ended, relatively unfocused and that can move freely between the client's communications and the content of the therapist's own mind and emotions. Freud (1923) referred to this as 'evenly suspended attention' – a kind of hovering over everything in the field of awareness. Bion (1970) has suggested it requires a state of mental 'reverie' and a willingness to stay with what is unknown or unclear, awaiting some pattern or form to emerge in either thought or feeling. This involves the therapist listening to her own 'free associations' to the client's material in a process that parallels the client's own task. The aim is to be open to unconscious as well as conscious levels of communication – to tune in to a level of private psychological processing that is usually screened out of the foreground of awareness – and in doing so to 'pick up' elements of this level of mental activity in the client.

From the client's point of view this means that she is not only being listened to but listened to in a certain way. The experience of both client and therapist is attended to seriously and in depth. Obviously the therapist is influenced by theory and established knowledge, but in the act of attending to the client this is put into the background to allow what is unique to that client and the present situation to emerge. This should be reflected in the content of the therapist's responses, which are more likely to be particular and personal than general or abstract. The language that she uses should reflect the vividness and immediacy of intimate disclosure and its unconscious roots. This quality of attention is also designed to convey a number of attitudes that the client may feel encouraged to identify with, and come to internalise as her own. These include interest in the content of her own experience and curiosity about the mental and emotional processes that surround it. The client may come to take pleasure in being surprising, even bewildering, to herself. The therapist's ability to attend to and reflect on the specifics of emotional life encourages a similar reflexive attitude and capacity in the client. The therapeutic situation thus becomes a space for thinking, which encourages the release and mutual exploration of more and more of the client's experience. It creates space in the client's mind too, transforming her capacity to be receptive and reflective. To the extent that the client is 'left alone', she is encouraged to develop her own resources. The therapeutic couple share the task of both undergoing experiences and thinking about them and this builds the client's self-analytic function.

Acceptance

The fundamental rule – to say whatever comes to mind – entails something of an injunction from the therapist and also asks for an implicit 'pledge' from clients: to be honest about themselves. This becomes an element of the therapeutic contract, but it also implies an 'ethic', a value that is to be sought, which is as much an outcome of therapy as its vehicle. Human maturity, Freud is implying, is the capacity to be fully, unflinchingly honest with ourselves, and to accept ourselves as we really are. In offering this context – and this pressure – for the client to talk openly and to reveal herself, the therapist is placed in the position of being a witness to whatever emerges. However, for the client, therapists are likely to appear much more like a detective seeing through her disguises or a judge weighing her value and her guilt. The fundamental wish to please or be liked will often colour the situation and lead to superficial compliance rather than genuine openness. Stronger fears may exist about what the therapist will think or even do in response to what has been 'exposed'.

Fears of this kind can easily be transformed into premature termination of the therapy or denigration of its value. This way the client can take the judgemental position and avoid the risk and vulnerability associated with real personal disclosure. To some extent these kinds of reaction are the stuff of psychodynamic work and can lead to useful analytic exploration. On the other hand, there is a powerful releasing and deepening effect associated with establishing trust in the therapist and actually experiencing her receptivity to and acceptance of areas of experience that are normally very private. This can be conveyed and established in a number of ways by the therapist: the confidential structure and boundaries of the work create a context where disclosure is formally protected and seems socially sanctioned; the professional training and relative anonymity of the therapist provide some expectation that the response received will not be personally critical or moralistic. But what does the therapist really think as an individual and how does this impact on the client? In practice the therapist's curiosity, her desire truly to understand, tends to mitigate the tendency to judge or condemn – it involves coming close to the client's reality rather than stepping back into a purely objective position. On the other hand, such acceptance does not necessarily involve agreeing with the client or reassuring her that there is nothing to be concerned about – in fact, it is acceptance with a sharp edge. Acceptance that is unquestioning may seem desirable but can, in some ways, be rather superficial and even seductive (Symington, 1996). The client's desire to be known and accepted in depth requires from the therapist an attitude that combines genuine acceptance with a deeper curiosity, a more thoughtful and sceptical element that actively challenges the *status quo*. The therapist is always attempting to make new sense of what the client is expressing, not just accept her current version of things. As the client comes to be able to collaborate in that endeavour, a deeper, more authentic form of trust is constructed.

The therapeutic setting

The relative passivity, attentiveness and acceptance that a therapist demonstrates need an appropriate context for their effects to be realised. The boundaries and rituals that frame the therapeutic work provide this. The arrangements of the physical setting as well as the culture of practice also have an impact. Clearly, effective therapeutic work is less likely to take place in physical setting that isn't conducive to it: the main requirements are for a space that is private, where there will be no interruptions and that is reasonably comfortable. While the practical necessities are obvious, the psychodynamic approach also places considerable emphasis on their symbolic function: they stand for reliability, safety and respect for the exploration of subjective reality; this, they say, is a special, protected space where something different can happen. Traditionally psychoanalysis is practised with the patient lying on a couch and the analyst seated behind them. This creates an atmosphere and setting particularly conducive to almost dream-like free associative expression (and intensifies other change processes such as transference and regression – see Chapters 5 and 6). Briefer and less intensive forms of psychodynamic therapy and counselling are normally conducted with both parties sitting in the more familiar manner in comfortable chairs and in unobtrusive view of each other. The use of the couch or the chair should be considered in relation to the needs of each individual client – what best enables her to achieve an appropriate expressive and exploratory relationship with the therapist and herself.

What applies to the therapeutic space also applies to therapeutic time. Clarity and consistency about the frequency and duration of sessions imposes a framework that allows for differentiation of sessions from everyday life in a predictable rhythm. This defines and contains the sessions – there is a sense in which the therapeutic hour takes on special, almost ritualised, significance by being so set apart from everyday reality (see Chapters 7 and 8). It makes it possible for both the therapist and client to enter a different mode of relating – perhaps a different state of consciousness – and to return from this at the end of the hour even when the experience becomes disturbing and intense. As Hoffman (1998) argues, the interplay of ritual and personal spontaneity in the therapeutic process can help generate a productive tension that promotes constructive analytic work. Because of these ritualised and symbolic meanings associated with the therapeutic frame, any disruptions – even predictable ones like holiday breaks or agreed changes in session times – are likely to carry real significance in psychodynamic work, whereas in many other therapeutic approaches this impact is frequently downplayed. Therapy is viewed as a unique and specially configured situation, not something to be treated as an everyday encounter within familiar but flexible patterns. Changes to any of its arrangements are thus powerful influences on both the experience and expression of clients.

Box 3.2 Case Example – Part 1: Expressing Feelings

Stephen came for a psychotherapy assessment shortly after his fortieth birthday. His family doctor had suggested this after he had made a series of consultations at the surgery for minor physical complaints and 'work-related problems'. The doctor was concerned that he was taking increasing time off work and suspected that this might be impacting on his marriage. She had prescribed anti-depressant medication but Stephen had declined to take it and appeared to be increasingly negative and withdrawn.

Stephen arrived early for his first appointment. He sat anxiously in the waiting room and immediately apologised for bringing two large briefcases with him as his female therapist showed him into the consulting room. He explained that they contained work he was taking home because he was under pressure to complete it as soon as possible. Without pausing, he went on to say that he might be wasting the therapist's time as he had a short period of counselling two years ago, adding that he felt the counsellor had soon become impatient with him. After this there were a number of awkward silences until the therapist commented on the uncertainty Stephen might be feeling in the session about the amount of therapeutic time that would be available for him.

Following this comment Stephen visibly relaxed. He found himself warming to his therapist; he had initially been uncomfortable by how little she said but he now had a sense that she was listening to him closely. He agreed time was an issue and talked at length about the unreasonable demands that were made on him in his work within the IT industry. He no longer enjoyed the work and had a struggle to get up to face the day. He talked negatively about the culture of his firm and gave an example of how he had been turned down for a promotion a few months ago in favour of a younger man whom he had been mentoring. He insisted he was still close friends with the man and bore no grudges but felt that the system was unfair and that he was undervalued.

Although the therapist continued to say relatively little Stephen felt she had understood him, particularly when she used the phrase 'bitterly disappointing' when reflecting back something he had said. He found himself talking freely about his marriage in a way that he had not expected. His wife didn't seem to have much time for him now that they had a young baby. He nodded vigorously when the therapist suggested that he might be feeling left out and to his surprise put his hands to his face and began to weep profusely.

By the end of the session Stephen had regained his composure. He felt drained but definitely relieved and expressed gratitude to his therapist for showing so much interest in him. The therapist felt a little uncomfortable about this but did feel a genuine sense of compassion towards him. They agreed to meet for two more sessions before making a decision about ongoing work.

The impact and limitations of expression

The boundaried and ritualised nature of the setting and the therapist's relative passivity, special attentiveness and accepting but searching attitude all combine to encourage a freedom of expression and opening up which can sometimes lead to a quite rapid sense of change and therapeutic benefit for the client (see Box 3.2). However, we need to guard against the idea that there is some perfect or ideal attitude for the therapist to adopt because this will militate against the spontaneous responsiveness that helps to vitalize the relationship (Lomas, 1994). Encouraged to talk freely in the presence of an attentive listener, people are often surprised at how much they reveal in therapeutic sessions, sometimes even against their conscious intentions. They may give voice to previously unexpressed thoughts and feelings or rediscover memories or experiences, the importance of which they have long since forgotten. As emotion is expressed and events recalled, a cathartic process can take place that feels immediately freeing. The act of sharing experiences that have aroused guilt or shame can also be profoundly relieving. Such experiences can grow out of all proportion when they remain hidden, perhaps fuelled by fantasies of what other people would think 'if only they knew'. Revelation and disclosure can then be normalising and lead to a greater sense of external perspective and more realistic standards of self-judgement. In addition, the simple act of giving expression to preoccupying concerns and difficult experiences can encourage some detachment from them and allow for new possibilities to enter the mind. In all these processes it is usually the case that some painful emotions have to be experienced and expressed before any relief is obtained. There is a sense in which things have to get at least temporarily worse before they can begin to get better.

Research on the expression of emotions (for example, Pennebaker, 1997) does seem to suggest that valuable changes can occur in some of the relatively simple ways outlined above. However, there are a number of reasons to be cautious about how significant and lasting this can be in more complex situations. It is certainly true that cathartic release can break the hold of a fixed emotional state, but often the processes that have led to the emotional strangulation will gradually reassert themselves. This seems particularly true if the emotional release is blind, that is strong emotions are expressed but without any real understanding or recognition of their meaning and relationship to other factors. In fact, just venting emotions can sometimes serve to reinforce them in the longer term rather than truly release them. This is particularly true if they are accompanied by patterns of conscious or unconscious ideas that sustain them but which go unexamined.

There is undoubted relief in the confessional process but unlike the church, a therapist offers no religiously sanctioned absolution. Whatever the merits of this process in religious terms, in psychodynamic psychotherapy interest is focused on the psychic processes that underlie it. Confession may achieve little more than a 'transference cure' with the therapist functioning only to moderate through her presence the client's own punitive fantasies rather than to genuinely change them. The reality is that guilt and shame will recur and that there may be a need to take sustained responsibility for a whole range of processes that have previously been pushed much further from awareness. Confession has its place but the attitudes and unconscious processes that accompany it are of greater therapeutic interest. If the individual remains excessively self-critical or self-conscious, she will continue to suffer. If she continues to need the reassurance of 'forgiving' authority figures, she remains vulnerable in future relationships. Change at these levels may need the release of feelings of guilt and shame but also intensive work to make sense of what is taking place actively to perpetuate them. This is unlikely to occur as a one-off event – it needs time to address.

Other problems with the simple idea of release through expression arise when the process of unburdening the mind becomes essentially the equivalent of 'dumping' or getting rid of a painful reality rather than of confronting it. In this situation, therapy can become a place to deposit experience rather than engage with it and the therapist can quickly feel quite burdened while the client is only temporarily relieved. Rather than experiencing things fully and with increased awareness, they are discharged and disowned. This type of process usually takes place at some cost to other people. It is an attempt at elimination rather than integration and actually depletes the client rather than strengthens her. Contrary to some naïve views, psychoanalytic ideas do not sanction total freedom of expression regardless of the consequences. In fact, plunging too directly into disturbing states of mind can lead some people to experience such intense and confusing emotions that they can feel overwhelmed or lose the capacity to function adequately (see Chapter 6). The therapeutic relationship needs to be sufficiently well established and the client sufficiently robust to be able to contain and manage such experiences. This requires careful judgement rather than blind faith in the idea that releasing the mind and emotions is unquestionably a good thing.

The release achieved through verbalisation, catharsis and confession can undoubtedly bring relief and some degree of increased freedom, but in many cases the benefits may be short-lived or superficial unless more fundamental psychological change is promoted in other ways. Problems tend to repeat themselves in recurrent cycles under the influence of dynamic factors not amenable to change through expression alone. In some areas, powerful obstacles or resistance to open expression can appear which demand closer examination and understanding. From the client's point of view the need to 'get things off her chest' should be supplemented by a desire to make more sense of her experience and to find some meaning in what emerges. The need to seek change through understanding and integrating experience thus comes to the fore. The gradual development of the capacity for self-reflection and for being in touch with oneself at depth is the greatest contribution that expression – and free associative expression in particular – makes to the emergence of fundamental and lasting change in psychodynamic therapy.

Conclusion

Therapeutic change is undoubtedly dependent on processes that release the mind and allow for some active expression of thoughts and feelings. Indeed, we seem to have a powerful need to express and represent our experience in some way. Without this the development of understanding and meaning is not possible. Discharge of emotions can bring relief, which, even if only temporary, may be crucial in establishing some faith in the process of therapy. This is particularly significant in the early stages where the working relationship is being established. What is also being established at this stage, however, is a reflective attitude which looks beyond the content of experience to its meaning. The interplay of expression and meaning is a key ingredient of psychodynamic change and makes it more extensive than is possible through emotional release alone. This is the focus of the next chapter.

Understanding, like expression, seems to be something we are designed to seek. This impulse is reflected in our desire to learn about and make sense of the world around us. Psychodynamic therapy harnesses this and applies it reflexively to our own actions and experience. Indeed, the wish to understand oneself is often an important motivation for people to enter psychotherapy. As the Delphic injunction 'know thyself' illustrates, one of the highest values has long been associated with self-knowledge. And knowledge of oneself isn't neutral. It affects what is known: we are already changed by the fact of self-discovery. Self-awareness or understanding can be thought of as both a desirable outcome of psychodynamic work and as a direct means – for many therapists the primary means – of effecting change.

Understanding in psychodynamic practice arises largely from the activity of talking and listening that takes place in the consulting room. When people express themselves in this special context, particularly when they talk in free associative mode, more is always being communicated than is immediately apparent. Meanings and intentions are conveyed that lie outside awareness. Numerous non-verbal channels exist too, mediating subtle messages outside the range of conscious control. It was one of Freud's most significant innovations to recognise that all behaviour, including apparently accidental words and actions, is potentially meaningful. He proposed that many actions and expressions can be understood in terms of determining processes that are unconscious and that, by a careful reading of the language of these processes, an understanding of their 'latent' meanings can be arrived at. While this idea has been extended in various ways over the years, it is still a defining feature of the psychodynamic approach.

Insight and unconscious meaning

The process of understanding or interpreting the meaning latent in the material that emerges in therapy is central to 'analytic' work. Freud saw this as part of the broad task of 'making the unconscious conscious'. The therapeutic aim is to increase the range of conscious awareness, particularly with regard to our own mind. This has come to be referred to as the development of 'insight'. Encompassed in this term is the idea of becoming more aware of our own hidden motives and impulses, and more generally perhaps, of the dynamic processes that underpin all aspects of our behaviour. Developing insight already represents, in itself, a process of change. What was out of awareness has now entered into it: there is a change in the content, perhaps even the structure, of consciousness. There may be a change in the quality of experience, a feeling of clarity, say, replacing a sense of confusion. Gaining insight into a previously unconscious feeling or impulse may transform a somatic state or behavioural symptom into a directly experienced emotion. For example, a headache or obsessive preoccupation may resolve into a feeling of anger. It is such authentic connection – in-*sight* – to unconscious levels of emotional life that is the key vehicle for furthering change and development in psychodynamic therapy. The goal is to expand the client's awareness of the unconscious meaning of her behaviour and by enlarging her consciousness to provide wider options for choice and control in her life. To see the truth about ourselves is to grasp what is needed to become more free.

Psychodynamic therapy is thus characterised by its attempt to explore and progressively uncover the complex textures of unconscious meaning that are attached to what people say and do. How are such meanings to be found? As is well known, it started with dreams, specifically Freud's own: his seminal work on the unconscious was largely based on his self-analysis and, in particular, a close examination of the nature of his dreams. He famously described dreams as 'the royal road to the unconscious' (Freud, 1900). The idea that dreams, which arrive unbidden and without conscious intention, can carry meaning has a long and significant history across numerous cultures, although this competes with the belief (still prevalent in some 'scientific' circles) that they are meaningless, simply by-products of the mind's physiology during sleep. Traditional interpretations of dreams often point towards elements beyond the person – such as Gods or spirits – as explanations of their significance. The psychodynamic view that dreams are a product of the unconscious captures a similar sense of their source residing outside the boundaries of the conscious personality. However, one of Freud's most original contributions was his formulation of how 'dream work', the process that gives form to dreams, operates. He saw dreams as expressing an unconscious wish that was seeking expression but which was unacceptable or anxiety-provoking to the individual: this is the latent content of the dream. It exists unconsciously but needs to be disguised and transformed to manifest itself in a dream in a way that is not recognisable. Nevertheless, the unconscious still expresses the wish, albeit in an indirect, symbolic way, through the dream. If this symbolism can be deciphered, the latent meaning can be grasped and insight into the hidden motivations gained.

Following Freud, other approaches have been developed towards understanding the unconscious content of dreams, particularly within the tradition of analytical psychology founded by Jung who identified collective forms that he described as archetypes. The Freudian idea that dreams are always wish-fulfilling, rather than expressing anxieties and fears or more generally some other form of unconscious thinking or perception, is less prevalent now. However, the fundamental idea that dreams carry symbolic meaning and that unconscious processes shape this symbolism has remained accepted across all approaches (Rycroft, 1979). Detailed observations of dreams have been crucial to making sense of the way unconscious thinking operates. Freud labelled this 'primary process' thought, distinguishing it from the 'secondary process' that characterises conscious reasoning (see Chapter 2). Primary process operates in a way that contradicts rational logic and it is this that accounts for the strangeness of dreams: understand this logic and it becomes possible to translate their underlying meaning. The form of the dream work includes the condensation of ideas so that one element stands for several 'thoughts', the displacement of an idea on to something else, the symbolising of emotionally charged issues by other innocuous stand-ins, and so on. Freud thus thought of dreams as intricate puzzles which required a kind of psychological detective work to unravel their mystery. This vision of therapy as involving a process of 'decoding' has been very influential in therapeutic practice.

Dreams point to a more general truth about meaning and the unconscious that is the keystone of the psychodynamic approach. Essentially, this is that unconscious logic both underpins and deeply penetrates conscious thinking and behaviour. There in an effort to keep unacceptable feelings and impulses out of awareness so they tend only to emerge in disguised form, but this form has a symbolic structure derived directly from the way the unconscious operates. The existence of such symbolic form means that information is constantly being conveyed by many types of expression and behaviour; they can be thought of as forms of communication – albeit unconscious ones – which are open to understanding. All the material of therapy – stories, memories, associations, the course of the session itself – can be thought of like a dream to be decoded, mined for its hidden meanings. To arrive at this understanding requires a process of interpretation. The 'favoured' focus – what is felt to carry the most therapeutically significant meanings – has, however, changed over the years (see Box 4.1). In fact, the full scope for interpretation of any material may never be exhausted, partly because of the vast range of determining factors and hence meanings that may be condensed into any one dream, symbolic act or utterance ('over-determination'), but also because such symbols tend to create ever-widening meanings through generative links to other things. New meanings may be found at the same time as prior meanings are integrated into wider frameworks of understanding. One of the challenges of psychodynamic practice, especially in briefer forms of work, is to identify from all the possibilities available what is most salient, most helpful, most facilitating of change at any given time. This is often achieved through choosing to focus on the clearest connections that can be made with the main difficulties or conflicts the client is experiencing in her life.

Box 4.1 Psychodynamic Interpretation

The activity of interpretation – finding unconscious meaning in the client's material – has been at the centre of psychodynamic practice ever since psychoanalysis proper was born out of Freud's move away from trauma theory and the cathartic method. However, the focus of interpretation – what is regarded as the most important and therapeutically effective place to seek that meaning – has changed over time.

Initially, Freud modelled his interpretive work on the unravelling of dreams. Free associations, resistances within them, symptoms and accidents were all subject to an intricate process of decoding. They were thought of as a puzzle to be unravelled with the aim of revealing the unacceptable unconscious wishes that were latent within them. Over following years, this work of decoding was extended to include an understanding of the client's childhood past and, in particular, of the conflictual wishes, fantasies and experiences that were developmentally formative of the neurotic difficulties. Freud's great case studies (such as 'the Wolfman' and 'the Ratman') illustrate his skill and continuing fascination with the detective work of deciphering signs and traces. Freud thought of this as uncovering superficial layers of appearance to reveal the true meaning of the past, a task akin to archaeology. This interpretative focus has been characterised as a project of 'reconstruction'.

Resistance was also always a significant area of interpretive interest but, with the growth of Ego Psychology in the 1920s and 1930s, the analysis of the client's defensive structures came to the fore. The focus was less on symptoms or their historical roots than the total structure of the personality, thought of as largely made up of typical defensive patterns. Thus interpretation of defence became the mainstay of 'character analysis'.

The significance of 'transference' as a source of information had long been recognised (see Box 5.1) but in a classic paper in 1934, Strachey proposed that interpreting the transference that was alive in the session was the only truly 'mutative' interpretation – the one that really produced change due to its emotional impact in the present. This view became increasingly dominant and transference interpretation has remained for most psychodynamic schools the principle vehicle for therapeutic work, although significant differences remain about how and when this is most effectively done.

Conflict and repetition

Just as dreams can be understood as a compromise between the expression of unacceptable wishes and their disguise, symptoms or the specific complaints that bring people into therapy frequently have a similar unconscious structure. Someone can experience an acute tension between what they want to feel or do and what they find themselves feeling and doing. They may know that something, such as panic about going out of the house alone, is irrational, but nevertheless experience the fear intensely and feel forced to act in accordance with it. This struggle seems to reflect a deeper conflict going on in the mind that is being manifested in the form of this disabling contradiction. If insight into the unconscious situation can be achieved, leverage will be gained for change – the 'symptom' should be less compelling if its unconscious determinants can be brought directly into awareness. There is a difficulty to be faced, however: this situation has originated as part of an active attempt to avoid awareness of some experience or feeling; it is a way of 'defending' the personality from a source of distress or perceived danger. In other words, awareness or understanding is being actively obstructed. This paradox is at the heart of psychodynamic therapy. Understanding is constantly sought in the face of an often elaborate and persistent effort to avoid it.

The nature of this conflict was discussed in Chapter 2 and represented in a simplified way in Figure 2.1. The 'triangle of conflict' illustrates how unconscious conflicts between a hidden feeling, wish or impulse and some feared consequence give rise to the formation of defences that disguise the conflict and exclude it from awareness (Malan, 1979). Another way to think of this same situation is of there being an intensely painful and feared 'object relationship' in the unconscious internal world of the client; allowing this to become realised must be avoided at all costs. Some other form of relationship is then defensively substituted – and enacted in everyday interactions – to avoid the one that is feared. For example, someone may have internalised recurrent experiences of relating to people in authority in ways that prove to be shaming and humiliating; they then seek to avoid this through a compulsion to challenge authority and to reject what they feel are, or might become, belittling attempts to control them. These 'models' are not essentially different: emotional pain is avoided by substituting something that disguises the true internal situation. Any deeper form of self-knowledge requires access to the hidden feelings or fantasised relationships which give rise to these defensive patterns and which serve to maintain them as part of our character structure.

When defences are working effectively we are protected from distressing anxiety and are thus unlikely to feel in need of any help. In effect, they represent coping strategies, albeit ones that restrict our awareness. However, defences do impair our flexibility and limit our capacity to manage situations, particularly new or challenging ones. Even relatively well-functioning defensive structures can start to break down under situations of severe stress. Perhaps most significantly they lock us into patterns of relating to the world that are relatively rigid. One of the effects of rigid defences is the very strong tendency of old patterns of conflict and coping to repeat themselves. Such repetition points to a fundamental difficulty people often have in genuinely learning from their own experience (Bion, 1962). The fundamental reason for this is that to learn from our experience we need to have adequate access to it – we must confront the true situation before we can genuinely 'change our minds'. This is what we avoid, even at the cost of repeating painful and frustrating difficulties again and again.

In the context of interpersonal relationships, the impact of previously patterned forms of experience and behaviour are often very striking and disruptive. We frequently find ourselves reacting in the same intense ways to different people even when the immediate context doesn't seem to warrant it. Clients often present with a sense of being trapped in repeating the same old issues in their close relationships. Psychodynamic theory and practice has become increasingly focused on understanding this relational context, both past and present. Its developmental perspective makes clear how the experience of relationship is patterned by the past through an internalised world of relational configurations (see Chapter 2). The importance of early relationships to psychodynamic understanding is sometimes presented in a rather narrow way that simply seeks to account for current behaviour in terms of earlier relationships. Such reductive formulations have a limited capacity to effect change. In fact, they can sometimes amount to no more than the attribution of blame, either on to oneself or – quite commonly – on to others, usually parents. Any sense of current personal agency is thus disowned. Far more significant in therapeutic practice is the recognition that what is actively taking place here and now in the therapeutic relationship is similar – or even seemingly identical – to what has taken place in the past. In effect, the present appears to be patterned on the past. Psychodynamic therapy is sometimes seen as being preoccupied with the past, but it would be truer to say it is preoccupied with the present 'in depth', which includes the past within the present. The action occurring now might seem more appropriate and make more sense, if viewed in the context of a different, earlier situation.

The links that can be made between the past, the present and other relationships outside the therapy are captured diagrammatically in Figure 4.1. There are three contexts of relationship that are vital to understanding behaviour patterns dynamically: past relationships, particularly those with parents and other major care-taking figures or siblings; the current range of significant social relations that make up the individual's life space (particularly those that are intimate or otherwise emotionally intense); and that special current relationship to which we

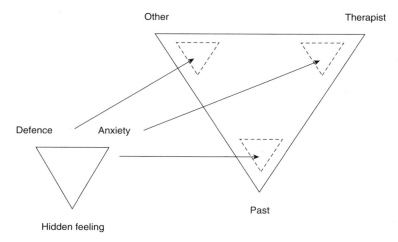

Figure 4.1   Combining the 'two triangles' (adapted from Molnos, 1984)

have direct access – the one with the therapist in the 'here and now' of the sessions. Malan (1979) proposes this as a second triangle (the 'triangle of person') alongside his triangular representation of dynamic conflict. However, Molnos (1984) has usefully combined these two triangles: in each relationship context the same conflict and defence configuration is being enacted. The underlying reason for the similarity of relationships across contexts is that the same unconscious dynamic structure is in operation.

What happened once in one place with one relationship is now happening here in quite another: the context is different but the same pattern is unfolding in it. It is as if an individual carries the original configuration with her to the new situation and is able to re-create it again in this new and externally different context. Her experience of relationships is to be understood as a relocation of dynamically charged relationships in the internal world into the external domain. This occurs through projection and unconscious distortion of perception so that patterns of behaviour reflect the internal situation more than external reality. Understanding or insight thus requires grasping that the difficulties experienced externally in current relationship are often shaped or even brought about by an internal reality being imposed on, or re-created in, the outer situation. If the inner world itself is not sufficiently open to change and modification in the light of 'reality testing', or if experience is always sought which tends to confirm our established ways of seeing things, it is inevitable that problematic experiences will be actively repeated again and again.

Interpretation

Understanding in psychodynamic work is designed to interrupt these compulsive or habitual patterns of repetition and provide room for greater conscious awareness. This creates a space from which different ways of responding can arise: the aim is to replace compulsion and repetition with a greater sense of freedom and spontaneity. To achieve this, the potential meaning inherent in all activity in and outside therapy needs to be open to enquiry – it becomes the focus of interpretation. Our immediate or conventional accounts of our actions cannot be taken at face value. Although at one level these may be true, they may well also be rather superficial – they fail to acknowledge unconscious factors that are at work in everything we say and do. An apparently rational explanation may be more of a rationalisation: plausible enough but designed to protect our conventional sense of ourselves. Interpretation is necessary to get beyond this superficial level, to address the latent meanings that may be present and to elaborate the wider meanings that could be relevant.

The combined triangle structure (Figure 4.1) is not merely abstract model building. It is a practical aid to the business of therapeutic interpretation. The triangles indicate the options and choices that a therapist might consider when seeking to assist the client to understand herself in a new light. They show how a therapist can make interpretations of the client's material in terms of both repetition and conflict. Thus with regard to illuminating unconscious conflict, we might choose to comment on the client's defensive activities, the anxieties which fuel them or the unconscious thoughts and feelings which are the occasion of those fears. For example, a client may have started to intellectualise when discussing an intimate relationship. The therapist could comment that her tone had changed when this topic was introduced, that it had become more emotionally distant. Alternatively, she might focus on the fear – say of being rejected – which she hypothesises the client is struggling with, remarking perhaps, that the client was trying desperately to cover over exactly this worry. Possibly – if this was relatively familiar ground – the therapist might speak directly to the underlying feeling, say of intense longing to be cared for which arouses her sense of insecurity and unworthiness, stating that 'we' know how much she wants this relationship and how much that scares her.

These 'technical' choices of what to focus on are made in relation to what the therapist believes the client can 'take on board': what she is striving to understand and what she can emotionally bear to know. Ideally, the new understanding that is being reached for should be close to the surface, within the client's grasp, just one further step beyond where she currently is. It should definitely not be obscure or esoteric. The client should be 'ready' for it – timing is crucial. Premature interpretations will be experienced as meaningless, unempathic and probably threatening – they will heighten resistance. The usual and safest sequence is to interpret the defences first, then the anxiety before addressing a hidden feeling. This starts from the 'surface' and goes deeper, but it is by no means an invariant rule. The choice of intervention is made on the basis of what keeps the client's anxiety within manageable bounds. The therapist needs to provide a context of support and containment to enable her client to sustain the emotional challenge which new understanding always entails, exposing her as it does to precisely what she has been afraid to acknowledge.

The triangle of person can also be of great assistance to the therapist's thinking. She is constantly attentive to themes – similar issues that come up repeatedly in different contexts. She will look for the underlying structure of the conflict in these situations but will also seek echoes and parallels across (and within) the three interpersonal domains. One context can be understood more fully in terms of another. Asking how current life difficulties seem to bear similarities to issues that had to be faced in growing up is the therapist's stock in trade – it is always a useful starting point. However, it is a helpful therapeutic tactic too. Framing understanding in the light of development makes it easier for people to acknowledge less acceptable aspects of their personality. By putting them in the context of the accommodations and adaptations that were necessary at an earlier time, empathy for a past self becomes possible: we see ourselves doing the best we could in the circumstances. Of course, understanding can flow in the opposite direction: how people currently feel and struggle casts light on how they may have experienced their upbringing. This is something that is often defensively obscured, for example by idealising or denigrating parents. The other domain of personal functioning – the therapeutic relationship itself – has come to be considered the most important of all in terms of change. Here information is first hand rather than filtered through the client's accounts: the therapist has direct experience of the client's conflicts and defences in the here and now of the session. More than this, the immediacy of the events 'in the room' makes them affectively charged so that the attempt to understand what is going on feels very real. Such 'transference interpretations' can have great power. They draw on the client's capacity to see that the therapist is actually different from what she had imagined – to reality-test unconscious assumptions (see Chapter 5). But this should not be to downplay the value of the other 'extra-transference' contexts of interpretation. Insight into the 'there and then' of external relationships past and present can have considerable value and draws on the client's capacity for curiosity about herself. A 'complete' interpretation addresses all aspects of the conflict in each of these contexts, but such an intervention is very seldom made except as a kind of review of understanding already established bit by bit.

Analytic interpretation in psychodynamic practice is too often depicted as rather mysterious and authoritarian. This may be because it is frequently seen as the unilateral prerogative of the therapist, which is exercised in occasional, profound but obscurely worded statements about the client. In fact, interpretation is better considered in more general terms as a process, actively engaged in by both therapist and client, of elucidating and finding meaning in the client's experience. As such it may involve elements of exploration, elaboration, confrontation, integration and formulation. What distinguishes a formal dynamic interpretation from these other interpretative activities is simply its form as an explicit statement that makes connections to an unconscious meaning. A client can make such interpretations for herself, although in practice this is difficult to do because of the defensive processes that cloud awareness – there is a need to gain some distance to be adequately self-reflective. The idea of interpretation can be daunting to the novice therapist who fears getting it wrong and so sticks mechanically to received ideas about what constitutes a 'correct' interpretation. In fact, the whole enterprise of making sense of the material a client presents is a highly fluid process in which the client herself needs to be an active participant.

Box 4.2 Case Example – Part 2: Initial Understanding

Stephen talked with increasing freedom in the second and third sessions with his therapist. He no longer appeared so anxious but began both sessions with a sigh and talked of feeling miserable and let down by the way his life was working out. He even acknowledged that there were times when he felt suicidal, but insisted he had no plans to act on this impulse. He would like to end his own suffering but would not do anything for fear of hurting his wife and baby. 'I must continue for them', he said in a self-denying tone, 'even though I'm not much good to them'.

He revealed that he had had a redundancy warning at work. On enquiry this appeared to be a general notice within the firm but Stephen was sure it had been posted with him in mind. He also disclosed that sexual relations with his wife had come to an end shortly after the birth of their child and that his wife had become very cold towards him. He said he didn't think this was her fault but that it was probably something to do with the demands of being a new mother. He said he just tried to do everything he could to support her.

The therapist asked about Stephen's early life but he gave a sparing description, insisting that his childhood was largely uneventful. His father worked long hours and was a rather distant figure whom he looked up to but never really got to know well. He died when Stephen was 23 from a sudden heart attack that Stephen put down to overwork. He described his mother as caring but always rather preoccupied with appearances and her own worries. He no longer had much contact with her or his younger brother as they both had emigrated. As a child he remembered looking after his brother a great deal and recalled being described as 'my right hand' by his mother.

The therapist felt moved by the depth of Stephen's unhappiness. Despite this she was vaguely irritated by his self-deprecatory manner and the sense of injustice that pervaded everything he said. She speculated that her reaction might reflect a level of anger and hostility that Stephen had difficulty in openly acknowledging to himself. Rather than interpret this feeling she commented on Stephen's apparent anxiety to look after other people. She linked this to Stephen's wife and childhood and also to herself when Stephen commented that he 'didn't want to burden her with all his crap'.

Stephen felt a deepening sense of rapport with the therapist and was beginning to value the sense of security and attention he felt in the setting of the sessions. When the therapist suggested that they could continue meeting weekly for therapy he was initially pleased but became unexpectedly concerned when she added that they would probably need to meet for at least a year and probably more. It flashed through his mind that she must think he was really 'screwed-up' and initially protested that he wasn't sure he would need this. However, he subsequently felt relieved to have been offered this level of commitment.

The construction of meaning

It might sometimes seem that psychodynamic interpretation is very much a theory-led activity, that there are established truths about the mind such as the Oedipus complex or unconscious envy which are the prime focus for interpretative understanding. Although theory does provide assistance to the therapist in making sense of what the client brings, the activity of meaning-making is in practice much more of a 'bottom-up' than a 'top-down' activity. Indeed, there is such a vast range of theoretical ideas that any imposition of meaning would have an obviously arbitrary quality: this is a parody of what therapy should be about. The only way of establishing what is of relevance is to stay close to what is observed and experienced from moment to moment with each individual. Bion (1970) advised therapists to listen to their clients 'without memory or desire'. This demands a state of mind which privileges the present moment and what arises in it over any preconceived ideas, preferred ways of thinking or wishes for the future. In this state, theoretical preconceptions are suspended and attention is devoted to what is unfolding in the session, including what is emerging in the therapist's own mind. It demands a capacity to tolerate 'not knowing' and wait for some possible shape or meaning to emerge. This means a willingness to listen openly to the unfolding narrative of the client as well as our own reactions to it, alert to possible links, patterns of meaning and features that seem to carry emotional resonance. It is far more a patient search for emergent meaning rather than an imposition of existing knowledge.

The style of the therapist's interventions should normally be tentative and open-ended: she is offering a hypothesis, an understanding that *might* fit, not an established truth. The therapist's posture is not one of certainty, although she does need to feel a degree of confidence in her efforts to discover the truth. How can the therapist know that an interpretation that she is forming is 'right'? In a sense the client is the 'teacher' – the source of confirmation or disconfirmation of the accuracy of the therapist's understanding. But the confirmation sought is not always direct and need not require the client's explicit agreement. Validation can come indirectly – the client's response offers further material that seems to elaborate the issue, or the emotional depth of the work is increased. Malan (1979) suggests that the effect of an intervention on the 'rapport' or emotional engagement between therapist and client is a crucial barometer of its accuracy. Correct understanding progressively deepens the therapeutic process. There is of course no 'objective' measure of interpretative accuracy. It is a matter of whether the client can use it to extend her awareness, whether it is subjectively convincing: Does it touch her? Does it 'fit'? Thus meaning-making in practice should have a dialogical quality. Rather than interpretations being formulated clearly in the therapist's mind and then given as a pronouncement, they often arise through a highly interactive process – the pursuit of themes, posing questions, seeking clarification and awaiting the response. In this way an understanding may arise in the minds of both therapist and client at much the same time, or an insight occur to one that can then be actively linked by the other to new areas, with interpretations which retrospectively amplify and integrate what has emerged. This can feel like a very creative process, with meaning being elaborated through the mutual participation of both parties.

In fact, this dialogical quality inherent in the process of meaning-making in therapy raises some profound questions about the nature of the truths that are being discovered. What is it that is being 'understood'? The therapist's posture – her starting point and method – is that everything is potentially meaningful, anything might be an unconscious communication. But 'unconscious meaning' is a tricky idea. If meaning is being progressively established in the therapeutic dialogue, perhaps it is not as pre-formed as was once thought. There are, in effect, two contrasting perspectives on the nature of meaning and understanding. One portrays understanding as discovering meaning in terms of a pre-existing (unconscious) reality – it is fully-formed, waiting to be uncovered and faced. The other views meaning as always being actively constructed and therefore never simply reflecting some objective state of affairs – it is a potential in experience waiting to be articulated. These are reflected in the different metaphors used about therapy. One sees analysis in terms of archaeology: an excavation and clearing away of material to find indications of what had gone before and so what underlies the surface situation: something else exists even if, in practice, its nature can normally only ever be partially reconstructed. The alternative, more contemporary metaphor is that of 'narrative', the construction of a new personal 'story', a coherent account which gives meaning to events (Spence, 1982; Schafer, 1992). Here the meaning is not in events themselves, whether internal or external, but in the story that frames them. This is always heavily determined by social context and the use of language, and in therapy, in particular, by the intersubjective processes and unconscious communications taking place within the relationship (see Chapter 5). Thus rather than being 'found', meaning is jointly constructed (see Chapter 8). This does not mean that it is arbitrary. There may be a number of different potential interpretations that give form to some aspect of previously undifferentiated experience, but they should be 'well-formed' – this is less an issue of 'accuracy' than of fit and scope. The two perspectives give rise to differing senses of how understanding may lead to change. On the one hand, we may imagine we are piecing together and courageously facing up to the truth in the hope that 'the truth will set us free'. On the other, we may believe we are piecing together an interpretative framework that expands and integrates our experience and makes sense of it in a coherent way: subjective meaning becomes pivotal. However, when we arrive at a new understanding it typically brings with it an experience of discovery or recognition, irrespective of whether this is understood to be through a process of revelation or an act of creation.

The value of understanding

If the discovery of new understanding is regarded as making such a crucial contribution to the process of personal change, what kind of change is it expected to bring about? There are several possible ways of approaching this question. Crucial to them all is the quality of understanding that is acquired. Although we have juxtaposed the idea of understanding with that of meaning, intellectual understanding doesn't necessarily make something *feel* meaningful. Some other quality is required. Usually it is said that only 'emotionally-grounded' understanding is associated with a valued experience of meaning. True insight should involve an immediate and potent sense of connection with problematic, emotionally charged, indeed painful aspects of experience. It is in no sense an intellectual exercise. Understanding 'builds bridges' to these elements of ourselves and includes them not simply in a new picture of our life but in a re-organised sense of who we are. This gives it the power of real meaning.

The experience of pain and distress is often accompanied by a profound sense that it is arbitrary and meaningless. Why can't we just be happy like other people seem to be? When we arrive at some understanding of our distress – place it in a context which gives it meaning – we may no longer simply wish to be rid of it but find that it is possible to experience it in a different way, one that actually helps us feel more in touch with ourselves. In a less powerful but no less significant manner, the confusing and apparently random pattern of our experiences can come to be viewed quite differently when brought together in a manner that establishes meaningful connections between feelings and events in both the past and the present. Meaning brings with it a sense of coherence and possibly the feeling that, in time, something further could emerge.

As we recognise connections between diverse aspects of our lives and actions, this understanding brings with it a much clearer recognition of what is going on within ourselves – what we are doing or intending or wanting or avoiding – usually out of conscious awareness. We may be able to come to recognise previously repudiated or unrecognised aspects of ourselves and thus begin the process of integrating these into a more inclusive experience of who we are. As we saw in Chapter 2, this is expressed in terms of the tripartite structural theory as 'where Id (It) was there Ego (I) shall be'. By knowing ourselves we are faced with a choice: to take personal responsibility in a new and expanded way. Understanding is not simply 'knowing more': the change is at the level of psychological structure more than content. Insight re-organises the internal world at a higher level of integration. This kind of structural change represents a real shift in our habitual ways of being and is seldom achieved through a sudden flash of insight. It is more likely to require a prolonged process of working through (see Chapter 7). However, understanding in its most literal sense of 'standing under', really coming to position ourselves differently in relation to some aspect of our experience, is a crucial aspect of any change to the organisation of the self. Taking ownership of parts of our self in this way can enlarge and strengthen the personality as it brings with it a lessening of defensiveness, greater flexibility, a clearer perception of both internal and external reality, access to new internal resources and a reduction of internal conflict. We have an expanded sense of our potential.

The very process of self-observation and self-reflection encouraged by psychodynamic work potentially leads to a profound alteration in self-experience and indeed experience of others. This has been described in terms of the development of a 'meta-cognitive' capacity to be self-reflexive. This is one of the mysteries of consciousness; it seems to go hand in hand with the development of empathic awareness of other people's mental states as well (Fonagy et al., 1991). Psychodynamic therapy cultivates the capacity for a finely-tuned awareness of the inner life both of ourselves and of others. Indeed, the position and activity of the therapist epitomises this sensitivity. Through an increased awareness of our own unconscious processes, the exclusive identification with our conscious personality is likely to be attenuated, while through identification with the therapist our capacity to adopt a position of self-reflective observation is strengthened. This increases our capacity for cognitive control, standing back from our experience and deciding how we want to act rather than simply *re*-acting. This process has many analogies, such as the mindfulness cultivated in some meditation practices; it seems to be associated with qualities of personal detachment, calm and well-being. In the psychodynamic world it is generally referred to as 'internalising a self-analytic function'. There is no beginning or end to the working of this quality of mind and it may well be one of the factors which contributes most to the longer-term benefits of dynamic therapy.

The limits of interpretation

Classically, in dynamic therapy, interpretation was largely based on what the client expressed in sessions. This made it quite dependent on the fundamental processes of free association described in Chapter 3. Inhibition of these processes would be viewed as a form of resistance requiring understanding in its own right. This places too much faith in verbal communication. As therapeutic experience has developed there has been an increasing recognition of the complexity and power of unconscious communication. It is now understood as functioning through often obscure non-verbal – indeed non-symbolic – channels. The client communicates states of mind without formulation in words, seemingly directly, in what is known as projective identification (see Chapter 5). These processes have become a crucial vehicle for understanding and interpretation in the context of the transference relationship. Without an awareness of this form of conveying meaning, therapeutic work can easily become just a 'talking-shop', cut off from its essential emotional and unconscious roots.

Perhaps the biggest single danger of an overemphasis on understanding as a vehicle of change is its potential to replace exploration and free expression and to act as a form of resistance to change itself. Having insight thus becomes something to claim or cling to rather than laboriously acquire through a continuing openness to what is *not* known. Intellectual insight can easily take this form and obstruct rather than inform the possibility of real change. The difference between an intellectual insight and an emotional one is the difference between simply recognising that our critical attitude towards someone might be fuelled by envy – let's say of their win on the lottery – compared to a realisation of this arising from the disturbing experience of our actual feelings of envy towards this person. The latter awareness is in no way theoretical or speculative. It is a direct and powerful experience that brings insight if it is accompanied by some conscious understanding of its nature. Accepting theoretically that I am envious can sometimes be a subtle way of avoiding experiencing it. In fact, unconsciously the feeling might be vigorously repudiated, allowing a conscious experience of critical superiority to remain: 'I'm critical of him because I'm envious – but I know it – clever me!' When understanding takes this form it needs to be recognised and interpreted as a defensive pseudo-insight in order to open up the possibility of real change taking place.

Although the therapist does not have an exclusive role in interpreting meaning, her position is still extremely influential. A number of possible problems arise as a result. Although we have pointed to the advantages of the therapist suspending preconceived ideas and general theories, it is inevitable that these will nevertheless shape what she sees or views as important. Many of us have the experience of reading a good book on clinical theory or attending a stimulating lecture and then, soon after, immediately finding certain elements in our clients' accounts that seem to fit with the ideas presented. In our need to find or create meaning we may be all too ready to impose whatever framework is shaping our thinking at the time. This requires constant vigilance, care to remain open to alternative meanings and sensitivity to the way understanding resonates or not with the client. If we are too attached to our ideas, we may subtly insist on them and elicit compliance on the part of the client rather than true insight. Indeed, some clients are only too ready to agree with everything the therapist says, a defensive posture that keeps things the same rather than achieving authentic personal change. Such compliance may also occur when the therapist is confronting strong resistance; this can lead her to work increasingly forcefully to overcome it. In such cases, her authority may eventually be accepted more as an act of submission than through genuine self-awareness. Therapy becomes more like coercion: even if the therapist's understanding is in many respects 'valid', the client's understanding is not. Change of this sort, based on the power structure of the therapeutic relationship, is a potential danger in all forms of therapy, particularly those in which the therapist takes a relatively directive stance or which ignore or actively exploit transference phenomena. On the other hand, it is equally possible to collude in not confronting certain issues even when it would be in the client's best interests to do so (Hinshelwood, 1997). In psychodynamic work the complexities of power and influence should be open to constant and careful examination.

Conclusion

In considering the discovery of meaning, the issue of the therapeutic relationship as a crucial vehicle for acquiring understanding has arisen repeatedly. This is true of the classical stance in which transference is a vital source of information that can lead to insight through interpretation. Taking a more constructionist perspective on understanding and change has a further impact on our sense of the importance of the position of the therapist in relation to the client as they co-create meaning. Throughout the history of psychotherapy there has been a question of what 'more' than interpretation and insight might be needed to promote change. The therapeutic relationship is the place where the answer has been looked for more than any other. Is it merely a vehicle for arriving at new understanding or is it a forum in which change is effected through the opportunity for new forms of relational experience?

Difficulties with personal relationships are among the commonest reason for seeking therapeutic help. Indeed, conflicts in the relationship with 'internalised others' are thought of in much modern psychodynamic theory as at the root of all psychological disturbance. Most theories of psychotherapy regard the therapeutic relationship as playing a crucial role in enabling change; a good 'alliance' is identified as the most reliable single contributor to change by numerous empirical research studies (Horvath and Symonds, 1991). The psychodynamic conceptualisation of the therapeutic relationship has been developed and refined over many years precisely because it is seen as one of the central elements of thera-peutic technique. It is among the approach's major contributions to the understanding of therapeutic change.

However, psychodynamic psychotherapy fosters a unique mode of personal relationship. This can appear unnatural, contradictory, and perhaps paradoxical:

- It is an intense personal reality that also has a quality of make believe, like a play being staged.
- It creates great closeness and a unique intimacy but also has a distanc-ing, even impersonal quality.
- It is intensely emotional but is also designed to promote thinking and rational reflection.
- It promotes an involving interpersonal experience in the here and now but is also understood as a re-creation of something from the past.
- It seeks to create something new and unique but is also viewed as repetition of the old and familiar.

Psychodynamic therapists see the therapeutic relationship as providing a unique opportunity for change but, unlike many other orientations which think of there being a natural, almost inevitable momentum towards transformation, they are very conscious that relationships both in and out of therapy can also be a way of staying the same. Change is something to be won through struggle within the unique context provided by a relation-ship with a therapist.

A psychodynamic perspective on the therapeutic relationship

Psychoanalysis began with Freud's analysis of himself. However, no one now thinks that we are likely to get as far as we might working alone in this way, no matter how truthful and astute we are. The perspective and involvement of another person in a special role is a crucial element in creating significant change. It is needed to bypass our self-deceptions and break up our habitual and simplistic ways of seeing ourselves. A therapeutic relationship is the vehicle for other change processes, a context that promotes and supports expressive catharsis and insightful understanding. In particular, it provides an immediate context for the communication and exploration of the relationship processes which are the source of our conflicts and limitations and so illuminates the lived reality which these difficulties give rise to. It gives the therapist direct access to the client's difficulties. More than this, however, it creates the opportunity for these to be resolved in the discovery of new ways of being with another person. It is itself a vehicle for change, an interpersonal experience with the potential to promote transformation. Much of the discussion on how to facilitate therapeutic change psychodynamically centres on the most effective way to utilise these various opportunities offered by the development of the relationship with the therapist. It is these issues that are the focus of this chapter.

A psychodynamic view of personal relationships suggests that they show consistent patterns for each individual, with similar themes linking different contexts. Unconscious conflicts and the defensive manoeuvres used to handle them underlie these patterns (as discussed in Chapters 2 and 4). They have their roots in the individual's developmental history and can be understood to reflect formative experiences and the ways that she developed to cope with them. These conflictual patterns are re-created again and again in new relationship contexts, including both the person's current life difficulties which brought her in search of help and also the place to which she has turned for that help: the relationship with the therapist. This idea is expressed diagrammatically in 'the triangle of person' (represented in Figure 4.1). Similar patterns of relationship and experience can be detected at each vertex of the triangle: the relationship with the parents and other significant figures in the past, relationships with other important people in the person's present day life, and the relationship with the therapist herself. This latter idea is the basis of the concept of transference. This is one of the crucial psychodynamic contributions to the theory of therapeutic change in general and is a central plank of psychodynamic therapeutic technique.

Transference

Being such an important concept, it is not surprising that the theory of transference has undergone significant historical development (see Box 5.1).

Indeed, it continues to be the focus of debate, as we shall see later in this chapter. This can be quite a problem for therapists. The fact that there are different perspectives and disagreement about meaning and emphasis can often be the source of misunderstanding and confusion. We shall try to tease apart classical from competing contemporary points of view as our discussion develops.

Features that identify aspects of a relationship as 'transferential' occur when perceptions, thoughts, feelings and actions are:

- repeated across various differing contexts in ways that are unselective and undiscriminating;
- inappropriate, tending to ignore, distort or actively transform aspects of reality in ways which conform to a fixed pattern;
- irrational, idiosyncratic, contrary to normal perception, emotionally charged and fantasy laden.

Such reactions are generally regarded as historically determined. In a sense, they are a repetition of the past in which an individual in the current situation is being experienced as 'someone else'. Thus transference is commonly thought of as 'transferring' the relationship with (usually) a parent on to the therapist. However, this is simplistic and can be misleading. It is better to think in terms of 'making real' in the present situation an unconscious pattern of relating developed from early 'object' relationships: what is transferred is some element of the person's current internal world on to external reality. Something is being relived, but it is not a faithful copy of past reality. Rather, it is the person's experience of it, subject to fantasy and distortion. (It is, for example, quite common for a client's recollections of the past and particularly her experience of a parent's character to change significantly during the course of therapy.) Thus transference is part of the experience of past and present alike, informed by the same unconscious psychodynamic processes. It is a regressive form of relatedness (see Chapter 6) which demonstrates the person's infantile conflicts and defences; it involves an archaic mode of representation which interferes with many current relationships and which gets drawn into the therapeutic situation itself.

Box 5.1 Transference

Freud identified the phenomenon that he called transference in the 1890s, at an early stage in the formation of his ideas about psychotherapy. He gave a detailed account in the well-known 'Dora' case study published in 1905. However, his understanding of the phenomenon and its clinical implications underwent significant development over the years:

- Initially transference was seen as a problem, a form of resistance in which the patient *replicated* past experience with parental figures with the analyst instead of the intended *recollection* of these experiences as memories. Transference thus defended against painful memories.
- By the time of writing his 'papers on technique' 10 years later, transference had come to be seen as an important and helpful tool in the analytic work in which the 'infantile neurosis' – the conflicts and fantasies of childhood – were re-evoked in the present-day relationship with the analyst. They thus became available for study and analysis. Transference was a source of data from which a *reconstruction* could be made of the patient's childhood experience.
- Over the next 10–20 years it was realised that this 'new edition' of old unconscious conflicts made them directly accessible, not simply for remembering and reconstructing but for re-experiencing and transformation through insight. Strachey (1934) called this process 'mutative interpretation' (see also Box 4.1). Transference was thus seen as the key vehicle of change.

As Freud first thought, resorting to this regressive way of relating in therapy is, in part, a form of resistance. It obscures painful experiences in both the past and the present by living out familiar and therefore safe (though often self-defeating) ways of dealing with them. Original traumas are repeated but in ways which are frequently problematic in the therapy, causing blocks to the work of exploration and understanding. These unacknowledged defensive manoeuvres need to be, in themselves, a focus of examination. However, these patterns are also full of information about the client and how she experienced her childhood predicaments. The client's internal dynamics, her 'inner world', are externalised and brought to life in the relationship with the therapist. We might say that the past is brought into the present and the outside world into the therapy room. The pain and confusion of childhood, the disappointments and defeats of everyday life are made real in the client's experience of the therapist. They are no longer being talked about but are being lived with a vividness and immediacy that gives the therapist direct access to what would otherwise be accounts and memories filtered through the client's selective perceptions. At the same time, because of the therapeutic setting, transference is never quite real; the ritualised elements of the therapy act as a 'framing' device so that it can be thought of as being like a play, a self-produced drama on the therapeutic stage. At one and the same time, it has the qualities of an intensely lived slice of life and a dress rehearsal of the real thing.

This access to the internal world in all its emotional and behavioural immediacy can be thought of as a form of expression or communication on the part of the client. Combined with its framing in a therapeutic context, the repetition embodies the hope with which the client came to therapy: that it would be possible to restructure these dynamics and find new meanings and expanded options with the help of the therapist. The hope is for a new and different kind of relationship. But the transference embodies the paradox of therapy: it brings alive the reality of the resistance to change. The client's energy becomes invested in making the potentially new just another copy of the old. As the therapeutic relationship becomes imbued with transference dynamics, the therapist is faced with the technical problem of how to make something new out of this re-creation of the old. This dilemma is also a conceptual one: if the therapeutic relationship is transferential through and through, what leverage can the therapist have to promote change? The traditional solution to this has been to identify other elements within the therapeutic relationship to provide a platform on which something new can be built.

The alliance and the real relationship

The therapeutic or working alliance is a psychoanalytic concept that has been generalised and widely applied across the full range of therapeutic orientations (Bordin, 1979). It is that element of the therapeutic interaction that is oriented to the work task. To the extent that the client is struggling with experiences that are resistant to these tasks – such as inhibition, self-deception and repetition – therapeutic change requires a mutual and collaborative intention to pursue these tasks and goals, in spite of the client's ambivalence about doing so. The resistance embodied in the transference is a particular stumbling block to doing this since it 'infects' and compromises that very collaboration and turns it into something different – a wish to be looked after, a fear of exploitation, a competitive struggle and so on. The idea of the working alliance suggests that there can be a 'benign split' in the client's ego: one part of her is caught up in the transferential re-enactment but another is available to join with the therapist in observing and thinking about herself. The capacity for rational collaboration is thus retained, separate and parallel to the disturbed part of the client that is caught up in a regressive and irrational transference repetition. There is thus an alliance between the rational, enquiry-oriented aspects of both participants, which holds the therapeutic process and keeps it on track. For the client, this means in practice that she communicates her experience and stays open to hearing the therapist's interventions and interpretations: she actively participates in keeping the processes of change alive.

The alliance is therefore a real rather than fantasy-laden element of the relationship – insofar as it is grounded in the rational therapeutic contract to work for change. However, the idea of a 'real' relationship between therapist and client (as opposed to the transferential one) has been used to refer to other elements in the situation as well (Stone, 1961). Each therapist has a distinctive personal presence, which inevitably demonstrates her ordinary humanness and her basic equality with the client as another individual in the world. This connects with the client's capacities for reality-based perceptions and interactions with the therapist as another person. It is embodied in those aspects of the relationship that are more ordinary and social. Clients often experience this equality as implicitly affirmative and encouraging. There is thus a real relationship, which is both grounded in a professional contract and also in touch with the personal dimensions of the human interaction.

This interweaving of dimensions to the therapeutic relationship has been highly controversial, both in terms of how it should be conceptualised and how therapists should most appropriately handle it as a matter of technique. The idea of the real relationship has been used to promote the need for therapists to show their warmth and concern for the client more openly and to adopt a more informal and spontaneous attitude as opposed to a strict interpretation of how the therapist's 'neutrality' should be expressed. It has been observed that therapists vary widely in their general professional manner – often irrespective of theoretical orientation – but there is intense disagreement about how to think about these differences. Indeed, it is debatable whether it makes any sense to separate off areas of the therapeutic relationship from transference dynamics. Freud (1912) initially suggested that there was a dimension of what he called 'unobjectionable positive transference' which carried the work of therapy forward, the essence of which is the respect and attachment the client has for the therapist. It clearly has unconscious and 'irrational' roots but it has been argued that so too does the supposedly rational, collaborative element of the alliance (Meissner, 1996). Much modern psychodynamic thinking returns to Freud in this sense, asserting that the idea of transference and the presence of unconscious dynamics within all relationships should not be narrowed: there is no sphere of interpersonal reality which is somehow free of or separate from its transferential roots in the inner world.

Corrective emotional experience

Bringing the client's problems alive once again in the relationship with the therapist would be pointlessly traumatic without the hope that something new could happen. This change should be more than an intellectual understanding of what is taking place. It should also involve an experience of a new and better form of relatedness. This goal has been called the 'corrective emotional experience'. Unfortunately, this term was originally proposed in controversial circumstances by Alexander and French (1946) and had rather a 'bad press' for many years as a result. Their book was important for initiating the idea of short-term psychodynamic treatment but proposed techniques for shortening the therapy that many regarded as dangerously manipulative. Alexander believed that it should be possible for the therapist to respond to the client's transferences by playing a role related to her projections and expectations but which was designed to provide a different and better experience. For example, a client with angry and rebellious attitudes towards authority based on an experience of an uncaring but controlling father figure might be assumed to benefit from the therapist presenting herself in an involved but permissive posture, providing a corrective form of experience that enabled the client to learn a new model of relating. This seems simplistic as an understanding of the complexity of change and both ethically and technically dubious in its promotion of an inauthentic and manipulative stance on the part of the therapist.

Nevertheless, as therapists have come to believe that a purely insight-oriented model of the change process is limited and incomplete, the term 'corrective emotional experience' has found favour again. There is general agreement that intellectual understanding is not all that is required for change, but rather a real experience in the present that has emotional depth and points the way to new possibilities. This would indeed be 'corrective' both of current distortions in the experience of other people and of the past experiences which are their foundation. However, the question of exactly what constitutes such an experience and how it should best be provided remains a continuing focus of debate.

In part, this debate is connected to the rival claims of 'conflict' and 'deficit' theories regarding the developmental roots of psychological problems (see Chapter 2):

- Conflict theories see change as resulting from the resolution or containment of dynamic conflict, which is typically achieved through a new understanding. The experience sought is that of the therapist's capacity to contain the conflict, rather than be drawn into it, and to make sense of it – for the client – in a transformative interpretation that expresses empathic understanding.
- Deficit theories conceptualise change as the repair of psychological structures that failed to develop optimally due to the absence of appropriate care-taking experiences. This is achieved by providing these opportunities for relationship again, through the therapist's provision of empathic resonance and holding, perhaps over lengthy periods. The client's developmental need for these forms of relating can then be redressed.

As can be seen, these theories differ on what the new experience is that would be corrective and seem to place different emphases on insight and interpretation as opposed to experience and new forms of relationship.

This difference in emphasis has been contrasted in terms of the client's *discovery of a new object* in the therapist's capacity to provide a different experience of relating, as opposed to the *discovery of an object relationship* that has always potentially been there but was defensively avoided in ways which the therapist casts light on. But perhaps this polarisation of approach is unhelpful. A more balanced position might suggest that the nature of the new and good experience and how it is created in the face of the tendency to repeat the old bad one may need to be different with different clients and at different stages of therapy.

The stance taken on the nature of the new experience that is thought to be required is influenced by the extent to which it is felt that the therapist's neutrality and distance do represent a viable therapeutic posture or whether the therapist will inevitably be drawn into an interpersonal exchange that reflects the client's world. There is a kind of circularity involved in psychological difficulties: people generally provoke the kinds of response which they expect from others, confirming their worst fears and replicating an experience of relationships which is not merely repetitive but has a self-perpetuating quality. Transference is thus not just a distorted perception. The client not only enacts how she felt neglected or traumatised or failed by her caretakers, but reproduces this experience in the transference by pulling the therapist into behaving in ways which seem similar. In order to find a way towards a new and better experience of relationship for the client, a therapist has to resist this gravitational force pulling her back towards repeating the familiar and to find a way out towards the discovery of a different experience. Clearly this is not entirely different from Alexander's original idea of playing a new corrective role, but it is much more difficult because it is not a 'set up': it is a process of real emotional engagement for both parties. These issues are at the heart of modern psychodynamic therapy (Mitchell, 1993; Caper, 1999). They are usually discussed under the headings of the therapist's countertransference, the process of enactment within therapeutic relationships and the meaning of the therapist's posture of 'neutrality'.

Therapeutic neutrality

The therapist's neutrality is one of the most important elements of the psychodynamic therapeutic posture. It emphasises what a peculiar activity doing therapy in this way can seem, since the therapist is enjoined not to do many of the things that would come naturally when with someone who is suffering, such as offering solace, support or reassurance. This 'abstinence' requires restraint and control on the part of therapists, the subordination of their normal human responsiveness. Freud offered various analogies for this, such as the surgeon's calm, unemotional focus on the task, or a mirror reflecting back what is observed without participation in it. These prescriptions for the therapeutic role serve a number of related functions. One is rigorously to guard the client's autonomy, avoiding meddling in her life, moulding her according to some image or imposing concepts on her. This is intended to protect the client not only from influence but also from being burdened with subtly meeting the therapist's needs. Of course, most psychotherapies are concerned to avoid any such charge of manipulation or imposition. However, psychodynamic theory is very alert to how difficult this is to avoid, precisely because of the power of the transference and the client's search for some guiding authority figure. Neutrality thus means not taking sides in the client's unconscious conflicts and in doing so crossing the boundary into a direct involvement in her life. In a conservative version of this view, awareness is the only proper therapeutic goal and the transference is to be analysed not exploited, even in ways that might seem on the face of it to be beneficial.

The therapist should be relatively anonymous in personal terms and subordinate her own needs and personality to the requirements of the role so as not to contaminate the interpersonal field. This aspect of the correct analytic posture is captured in the famous metaphor of the therapist as a 'blank screen' for the client's projections. The aim is not only to enable free expression (see Chapter 3) but also to leave an 'empty stage' on which the internal dynamics of the client can come to life in a form that is as unadulterated as possible. The client as it were 'hangs' her transference on to a neutral therapist – one who is just there doing her job! In particular, the therapist should not fall into the trap of embodying the transference figure existing in the client's fantasy. In this view, her principal task is to not join in the game: she should stand firm and not give way to the temptation to step out of role. Otherwise it will not be possible to distinguish the client's distorted perceptions from the therapist's own involvement.

The anonymity of the therapist is heightened in classical analysis by use of the couch, depriving the client of the opportunity to monitor the therapist's reactions through seeking non-verbal cues. But even in face-to-face therapy, the therapist's restraint, her lack of self-disclosure and unwillingness to answer personal questions, her refusal to respond in familiar and social ways or play expected roles to gratify the client's wishes, all serve to create a relational context that is largely undefined and which stimulates the emergence of the client's unconscious wishes and fantasies. The transferential situation gradually deepens and intensifies to become what is known as a 'transference neurosis'. This is a regressive situation (explored in Chapter 6) in which relatively undifferentiated 'infantile' conflicts come to the fore. However, it has long been recognised that this notion of a blank screen is at best an ideal: it is never actually attained. This creates a major technical and theoretical problem, which we will explore through the issue of countertransference, a concept that has come to occupy a central place within psychodynamic psychotherapy.

The therapist's countertransference

The term 'countertransference' is commonly used to mean two almost contradictory things (see Box 5.2):

- It is the most significant interference with the progress of therapy, resulting from the intrusion of the therapist's own emotional difficulties.
- It is the most helpful tool in the therapist's armoury, giving access to what is otherwise out of awareness.

In fact both of these meanings need to be kept in mind but the confusing terminology does not help!

Box 5.2 Countertransference

In a curious fashion, the concept of countertransference has undergone an almost exactly parallel process of historical development to that of transference but more slowly and over a much longer time scale.

- Countertransference was discussed by Freud in 1910 as an obstacle to the analyst's functioning with appropriate neutrality. Neurotic transferences towards the patient caused inappropriately hostile or erotic feelings, which had to be controlled for the work to proceed. Countertransference was thus seen as an impediment to therapy and it continued to be viewed in this way for several decades. Experiments in self-disclosure and mutual analysis by Ferenczi in the 1920s, which explored a different point of view, were poorly regarded.
- In the 1950s authors on both sides of the Atlantic, such as Heinemann, Little, Gittleson and Racker, suggested that the analyst's feelings towards the patient were a source of useful information, alerting her to aspects of the relationship that were otherwise out of awareness. Countertransference was thus a source of data about the patient's unconscious.
- In recent years, analysts have increasingly argued that a vital dimension of the therapeutic work is the therapist's own processing and transformation of her countertransference feelings. Writers such as Symington, Hoffman and Brenman-Pick see this internal work as contributing to change in the relationship and the client. Countertransference has thus come to be recognised as an important vehicle for the work of change.

Consider first countertransference in its original meaning – inappropriate, unconscious responses by the therapist, rooted in her own personal dynamics. These are likely to interfere with the exploration of the client's inner world through the inappropriate and confusing introduction of issues that do not spring principally from the client's own conflicts. In the classical model, this form of countertransference is a 'contaminant' of the therapeutic field. It is the source of a breakdown in the therapist's neutrality – she has been drawn out of role. At the very best, this distracts from the focus on the client's issues and the therapist's capacity to see and understand those clearly. At worst, it can result in the exploitation of the client – subtly or overtly – to serve the therapist's needs and unconscious agenda.

This understanding that the therapist's own conflicts can compromise the therapeutic relationship is a vital psychodynamic insight that has been acknowledged and incorporated in many other therapeutic traditions. It is one of the major reasons why both preliminary personal therapy and ongoing professional supervision have become accepted features of the culture of counselling and psychotherapy. The sheer difficulty of becoming aware of and correcting the impact of such countertransference responses remains a significant challenge in all therapeutic practice.

Countertransference as informative

Countertransference is not simply a subjective interference on the part of the therapist, however. It can also be seen as objective – a vital source of information about the client contained within the therapist's reactions to her. Such reactions can be a reality-based response to how the client presents herself and the interpersonal cues that she gives. These constitute invaluable evidence of how other people might also respond to this person. The strength of this approach is that such responses are often clues to subtle aspects of the client which would otherwise lie outside the therapist's awareness: they point to hidden features of the client's emotional world. Racker (1968) identifies two forms that this might take. In a *concordant* countertransference, the therapist identifies with the client's position and feels as she does. This capacity is the source of empathy and vital to the therapeutic process, but sometimes the feelings evoked by identification are not recognised as such. In a *complementary* countertransference, the therapist's experience is of being treated by the client as the 'other': she identifies with the client's internal model of how other people feel and act towards her. In a sense, empathy breaks down and the therapist becomes 'role responsive' instead (Sandler, 1976). For example, the client may present as weak, pathetic and deferential, making the therapist feel strong, helpful and wise. This process of role responsiveness is universal in human relationships: we constantly elicit responses from others that fit with our unconscious expectations.

These kinds of countertransference experience are often discussed in terms of the Kleinian concept of 'projective identification' (Ogden, 1982). This describes the process by which unmanageable experiences (or 'parts of the self') are evacuated and 'put into' another person by provoking that state of mind in her. Originally conceived by Klein as a manoeuvre within someone's inner world, Bion (1962) reconceptualised this process in interpersonal terms. The intensity of these experiences and the subtle, even mysterious, way in which such self-states are 'transmitted' to (or evoked in) the therapist are frequently observed in the practice of psychodynamic therapy. The idea of projective identification is often understood in terms of the communication of intense emotional states but Bollas (1987) points out how many subtle elements of the therapist's experience – fleeting thoughts or memories, images and passages of music – seem to be evoked in response to the client and can be thought of as countertransference communications, another feature of the idea of 'news from within' (see Chapter 3).

Countertransference experiences viewed in this light are a kind of unconscious communication from client to therapist. What is more they can often be thought of as carrying an implicit request – for the therapist to manage something for the client that she cannot do for herself. Thus a key element of the therapeutic relationship is for the therapist to 'contain' these projections, not to act on them or to defend against them but to experience the client's unbearable self-state and, in a further step, to process it emotionally, to make sense of it and so, in due course, to make it more manageable for the client. The therapist should thus receive these unconscious communications through an openness to and acceptance of her own internal experience before trying to symbolise them and communicate them back in the form of an interpretation about the client's disowned experience.

This understanding of countertransference as a form of empathic connection in which the client influences – even coerces – the therapist's inner life for purposes which are both defensive and communicative has been a vital advance in the subtlety and flexibility of psychodynamic therapy. It has extended the range of client transferences which can be productively managed. This approach to therapeutic understanding has now become so pervasive that there is a risk that countertransference experiences are misunderstood as states of mind solely evoked by the client. The original understanding of countertransference as stemming from the therapist's own internal world still has a vital part to play in making sense of the complexities of the therapeutic relationship. Indeed, it is in the area of the intersection of these two perspectives that contemporary debates about technique are most alive.

Box 5.3 Case Example – Part 3: Repeating Patterns

Over the first few weeks of therapy Stephen's mood improved significantly. His situation at work and at home remained the same and he continued to feel he was not being treated fairly but he became more optimistic and positive about himself. He thought the therapist both understood and liked him. He saw her as being on his side against the misfortunes he was facing and in touch with how difficult life could really be. He even disclosed to her something he had always vowed to keep a secret – the fact that his wife had previously had an affair. At the time this had wounded him deeply. He thought that he was partly to blame because he didn't want them to have the baby his wife longed for and went on to explain that he didn't want to bring another life into such a disturbed world. He believed his wife had the affair to make him appreciate her wishes and as a result he had agreed to try for a family. He confided his bewilderment that things were not better between them now that she had the child she wanted.

Over the next two months Stephen was full of praise and gratitude towards the therapist but seemed hurt and disappointed on a couple of occasions when the therapist forgot some details he had previously told her. The therapist felt slightly guilty about this and made a conscious effort to concentrate harder and take fuller notes after the session. She didn't feel entirely at ease with Stephen's positive comments but found herself working increasingly hard to live up to his expectations.

The therapist then took a break in the sessions at short notice due to a meeting that could provide an opening for her own professional advancement. Although she had the opportunity to tell Stephen in their session on the day when the arrangements were made, she completely forgot to do so and had to write to him to cancel their next appointment. Stephen seemed sullen and let down at their next meeting but told her that he realised it must have been something important and that he hoped it had been enjoyable for her.

The therapist felt both irritated and guilty and discussed her feelings in supervision, including an unexpected impulse she subsequently had to shorten the period of therapy due to his apparent improvement. She realised that she did not normally act in this way and that other dates would have been possible for the meeting but that she had readily accepted the date that clashed with Stephen's appointment. She felt that her failure to tell him in person helped her to avoid the reality of her own frustration and hostility towards him. She realised that she was acting from feelings of resentment about the idealised expectations she felt he had of her and her subsequent guilt for not living up to these. The supervisor suggested that she might be enacting a pattern that was similar to those Stephen experienced in relation to others and that this could be an important vehicle for understanding his recurring problems more deeply.

Participation in the therapeutic transaction

The idea of role responsiveness as a way of conceptualising the client's creation of a countertransference response in the therapist goes beyond the notion of creating an emotional reaction or a state of mind in the other person. It implies the active participation of the therapist in an enactment of the relationships in the client's internal world within the therapeutic relationship itself. The client pulls for a particular way of being which repeats something characteristic about her own relationships; the therapist responds in the expected way. The sense is that something is inevitably repeated between the therapeutic couple, not simply as the client's projection (staging a play with the therapist as audience), but something is played out in the present reality between them (the therapist participates, takes on her role in that play). The client thus actively re-creates her past – her characteristic experience of relationship – and the therapist is drawn in to it. The internal world is 'actualised' as part of a complex dance that takes place between the two participants. The therapist is thus no longer simply an observer of the transference, but is at best an observing participant: inevitably drawn, to a greater or lesser extent, into playing a role in the unfolding drama (Hoffman, 1998).

This challenge to the ideal of the therapist's neutrality within the interaction gathers force from the observation that the presence and personal participation of the therapist – unique and idiosyncratic as it inevitably is – probably plays a crucial role in the unfolding of the transference drama. On the one hand, there is the influence of the therapist's own unconscious dynamics – her 'subjective' countertransference to the client – which colours the way the transference is realised between them. The particular 'fit' between therapist and client at the level of unconscious dynamics will subtly (or not so subtly) alter the quality of the transference (Kantrowitz, 1996). On the other hand, at a more 'real' level, the therapist's character and personal presence has an inescapable impact on the client's experience. She always offers more than verbal interpretations: her tone and manner is meaningful, the way she brings to bear her own experience, what she chooses to comment on and how, always exerts some influence. The therapist has a constant personal emotional experience which engages her own vulnerabilities (not merely occasional 'subjective' countertransference distortions) and, crucially, the client senses this. In this way the therapist is always revealing herself: there is no hiding place in 'neutrality'. There is conscious and unconscious communication, not only from client to therapist but also in the other direction. The client's accurate perceptions of much of what the therapist does and who she is has to be taken into account. Our understanding of the relationship must become one of reciprocal influence, each shaping and responding to the other. This has come to be viewed by some thinkers as a key dynamic of the change process.

This critique of the classical position is now widely accepted but there is a spectrum of responses to it, varying from the conservative to the radical. A conservative position would suggest that although the therapeutic interaction is a joint creation, transference can still be thought of as something separable, with a momentum of its own that is imported into the therapy by a client who is rigidly compelled to view relationships in a certain way. While enactments happen, their frequency varies and this is partly dependent on the skill of the therapist in being able to resist the temptation to be drawn out of role; being flexible is equivalent to yielding to temptation or caving in to pressure from the client. While neutrality is only an ideal, it is a helpful one, enabling the therapist to remain relatively free of countertransference actualisations or at least to endeavour constantly to purify the therapeutic relationship of countertransference involvements. A more radical view suggests that there is no way to reduce many aspects of the therapist's involvement and so therapeutic theory and technique must be revised to accommodate this new understanding. Again there is some value in both views: it makes sense to think of there being a continuum of relative contributions from therapist and client and that this may differ depending on the maturity of both parties. But the more radical view is in tune with a wider context of developing theory and so its implications for therapeutic change need to be explored further.

The therapist's availability in the transaction

The idea that the therapist's involvement cannot be eliminated due to the constant and inevitable bi-directional influence of the participants on each other, at levels outside awareness, means that there is always going to be a degree of transference/countertransference enactment pervading the therapeutic transaction. An 'interactionist' or 'intersubjective' perspective suggests that this simply has to be accepted rather than fought against (Renik, 1993; Ogden, 1994). There is a kind of subjective sharing of experience and a co-creation of meaning between the two participants through their actions, interpretations and reactions. Thus both transference and countertransference are jointly constructed; the boundaries between transference and countertransference and between transference and reality become very blurred. While the client may select, exaggerate and distort, she does so in ways connected to the therapist's real participation at both conscious and unconscious levels. She integrates her experience of the therapist, in plausible ways, into her own system of meaning. The transference is thus a blend, a complex alloy of the past and the present, the real and the fantastic: it is not a dichotomy. Everything in the therapeutic relationship is both real and transferential.

While this interactionist position might seem disorienting, leaving the therapist no solid ground to stand on, it opens up some liberating and creative perspectives for the creation of change through the medium of the therapeutic relationship. If neutrality is an unrealisable ideal, perhaps participation in the therapeutic re-enactment must become the key dynamism for change. Champions of this point of view (Mitchell, 1988; Hoffman, 1998) suggest that the classical model, or conservative reinterpretations of it, simply fails with many clients who are unable to tolerate and use that strict framework. Even for many who can use it, the therapist's reserve can distort, inhibit or diffuse the development of a full range of transference engagement. The ideal of neutrality can become a resistance by the therapist to knowing her countertransference and this forecloses the client's opportunities to get in touch with what she needs to experience. The therapist has to offer herself as the necessary point of attachment for the transference, otherwise neither party is fully engaged with the therapeutic process and depth is lost. Freud's original idea of the unobjectionable positive transference carrying the therapy may be closer to this idea than the overly rational concept of the working alliance. It suggests a different therapeutic posture in which the therapist accepts her entry into the client's relational matrix and allows herself to be recruited as an 'accomplice' in the re-enactment which the client constructs. By being able to occupy to some extent the countertransference position offered, she can understand the client's world from the inside. She surrenders to being used and shaped in the service of a deepening of the other's experience of herself. The goal, of course, is to make something different happen as an outcome.

Technique and the therapeutic transaction

There is a spectrum of ways of understanding how therapists should conduct their work from the light of this changing theory – from the conservative to the radical. The theory of technique has been particularly slow to change historically: there is a strong 'analytic superego' that is deeply suspicious of deviations from accepted procedure and fears that, in Freud's terms (1910b), these represent 'wild analysis' that lacks discipline and hence is unsafe. The blank-screen version of the therapeutic posture has shown exceptional resilience in the face of theoretical challenges to it: not revealing personal details or answering questions remains the therapeutic norm. By contrast, radical critics suggest that whatever the therapist does – remaining silent, withholding information, even taking time to think – always means something to the client, always has an impact: there is no way *not* to act. Therapists, therefore, cannot avoid their inevitable influence. On the one hand, they must include the impact of their participation in the therapeutic enquiry. On the other, they must accept that they will be seen as mentors and cannot escape the responsibility of trying to act with wisdom (Hoffman, 1998).

If a simple understanding of neutrality is no longer tenable, the issue of what constitutes therapeutic discipline has to be rethought. A conservative stance is for the therapist to be constantly distancing herself from the enactments in a way that impels the client to be aware of her contribution. The emphasis continues to be on observing how the client transforms what the therapist has said or done, drawing attention to how an interpretation is experienced as a suggestion of how to be. More radically, there needs to be a constant interplay – a dialectic – between participating in the therapeutic interaction and monitoring and understanding it. Flexibility, a range of options of relatedness and openness to the client's impact should take place against the backdrop of the discipline of constant reflection and the subordination of the therapist's wishes to the client's long-term interests. There should be an ongoing critical scrutiny of the therapist's participation: if the rules of technique no longer give clear guidance on the 'right' thing to do, the therapist needs to worry about everything that she does! She never knows the full meaning of what is taking place and it is inevitably personally expressive in ways that are not transparent to herself. The therapist's commitment (and her skill) is to facilitate the ongoing enquiry into what is taking place between the two participants, to foster reflection in both. This requires confidence in the analytic method and in herself but there is no source of certainty.

Framing therapy in terms of an intersubjective transaction highlights some of the strangeness of the relationship. There is an odd kind of mutuality about it; it is intimate but asymmetric. The therapist is a person like the client; she does not have a monopoly on sanity. But it is a hierarchical situation in which the therapist is given greater power and authority. This is inevitable because she generally has superior knowledge of the situation, is charged with having a special concern and regard for the client and adopts a position that promotes the more positive elements in her personality, while the client is invited to engage with the less integrated parts of herself. This hierarchical 'gradient' within the transaction is vital. The therapist's restraint communicates that the therapy is for the client; it places limits on the therapist's impact but the authority it confers makes her participation matter. The therapeutic frame creates a context that provides some reflective space; it gives the transaction an element of transparency, making it a transitional space, an arena for creativity (see Chapter 8).

Table 5.1   Conservative and radical views of the therapeutic relationship

Conservative	Radical
Transference is a process with its own separable momentum in the therapy.	Transference is part of an inevitable bi-directional influence that takes place outside either party's awareness.
The client is rigidly compelled to distort the meaning of the process in characteristic ways.	There is a co-creation of meaning and a sharing of experience between therapist and client.
Technique is to observe and comment on these distortions.	Technique should be revised in the light of this co-creation.
Participation by the therapist in enactments does take place but their frequency depends on her skill at avoiding it.	It is not possible to reduce or avoid this kind of involvement by the therapist.
Flexibility of posture and technique is unhelpful and collusive.	The therapist should be open to the client's impact and be available for a range of options of relatedness.
Neutrality is an ideal but a helpful one.	Therapists should accept this participation in order to gain access to the client's world.
Therapists should constantly purify the relationship of their countertransference involvement.	Therapeutic discipline is in the scrutiny of and reflection on this participation.
By distancing herself from enactments the therapist compels the client to be aware of and take responsibility for their own contribution.	There is a dialectic between participating and understanding that is created between the participants. The therapist can never know the full meaning of the interaction.

This understanding of the therapeutic interaction does not make the task any easier. Being able to disentangle herself from the transference/countertransference matrix is a crucial and difficult act for the therapist. There may be a sense of danger or an inability to think, an experience of being paralysed or trapped in role. These are likely to stem from the theraspist's own most painful and problematic issues becoming caught up in a fused way with the client's, so that her own sense of sanity and worth is eroded. The experience of stuckness or 'impasse' may be a crucial moment in the process of transformation (Leiper, 2001). The therapist has to re-establish her sense of boundaries, staying in touch with the client's experience while asserting her own presence and perspective. This entails what has been called an 'act of freedom', an internal move by the therapist out of a fused state of mind into one of greater clarity and separateness (Symington, 1983).

Processes of change through relationship

It is common to feel a lot better after entering therapy, often quite quickly. The psychodynamic tradition tends to think of this in terms of a 'transference cure' and is deeply suspicious of it. It is understood as a function of the power of identification of the therapist with an idealised figure in the client's internal world, typically a reassuring or nurturing parent. There is a constant pull in the direction of idealisation within the therapeutic relationship at all stages of its development and many other forms of therapy seem to work on the basis of fostering it. By doing so, however, they maintain a split in which painful experience is denied and located outside the relationship and the self. This is a position of familiar safety for both parties but promotes an unstable and frequently a damaging solution – lasting change depends on the integration of disowned experience, the resolution of conflict and the building of psychological structure. By challenging the familiar configuration, psychodynamic therapists enable other, more difficult elements to emerge into the relational field where they become available for transformation. The paradox is that part of what brings the client into therapy is just these fantasy-laden hopes of a magical solution provided by an idealised figure: they provide a platform for the therapeutic relationship yet its project is to dismantle them. The therapist must use the authority embodied in the asymmetry of the therapeutic relationship to engage these fantasies of her omnipotence – but not collude with them. Her authority is an 'ironic' one in that its goal is to deconstruct or dismantle its own basis in favour of a relationship which is more real, less driven, more limited but less constricted.

For this to happen, the client who is actively re-creating and repeating the past must also be doing so with a healthy, developmental wish to create a new outcome. Old ghosts are invoked and let loose in the transference in the hope that they can be laid to rest. Reliving old patterns in the therapy is pointless in itself – to some degree it happens everyday! However, the artificiality of the therapeutic situation can allow openness to deeper experience and a taking of risks. The context makes the pattern of repetition clear and vivid; it becomes transparent and so already, to some extent, different. There is an interplay between repetition of the old and familiar and discovery of the relatively new emerging within the old ground. By opening up experience in this way, through her emotional availability and thoughtful curiosity, the therapist enables a new experience to unfold which alters the inevitability of past restrictions. The client comes to appreciate her own role in re-creating familiar disappointments and is helped to take responsibility for this. It is only possible for her to stop ridding herself of unbearable elements of her experience and deflecting her sense of 'blame' on to others, through the involvement of a therapist who accepts and contains these experiences and who, in addition, works to free herself from the coercive pressures which the client unconsciously exerts.

Although this has classically been thought of as helping the client to find her own 'inner truth' through an exploration of the therapeutic transaction, it may be more appropriate to see it in terms of opening up available options about how to relate. The therapist creates opportunities for the client to view her experience in other terms through her presence and availability, her ability to manage a range of experience, the atmosphere of respect and concern communicated and her steady, even-handed curiosity to understand the client's world. As another person discovers us, so we can discover ourselves. Thus the process of enquiry is crucial in its own right. It establishes a process of negotiation about the meaning of the therapeutic relationship, which respects each person's experience and demonstrates the capacity to recover this when it gets lost. The therapist mediates openness towards what is other than herself, a willingness to be affected by it and to take risks. The client identifies with the therapist's curiosity and her sense that experience can be borne and given meaning. Something is learned that cannot be taught but only acquired through participation in a relationship. The client develops a new capacity for relating, not only to others but also to herself.

Conclusion

Expression always implies an imagined audience: it is always communication. In the context of therapy, this constructs, with the help of the therapist's responsiveness, a relational matrix. Interpretation, as an action designed to discover meaning, not only creates symbolic links which integrate dissociated elements of a person's inner world, it also builds links between two minds – it is a bridge between the experience of the therapist and of the client. The therapeutic relationship is not only the medium of communication and understanding, it is the necessary vehicle – the crucial link – in the whole change process. What is most deeply personal is arrived at only in relationship with others. The presence of the other allows us to come into contact with areas of experience that are hidden, disowned or poorly articulated but which carry the seeds of transformation. This process of coming into contact with ourselves at depth is the work of regression.

The process of change is often described as a journey and psychotherapy can be thought of in terms of a quest – a search for an elusive prize. The motif of the quest is pervasive in the traditional tales of many cultures, their myths, legends and fairy stories: a hero is sent on an apparently impossible errand to find something hidden or lost or guarded or paradoxical. He (usually!) must face many obstacles and trials and travel beyond the everyday world before returning home with what has been won. This narrative has commonly been understood as representing the path of personal and spiritual development, the search for the true self or soul. Psychodynamic psychotherapy is often figured in just this way: the client is guided on an interior journey to find what is hidden but of ultimate value within themselves.

This interior journey is pictured by psychodynamic theory in two closely related ways. One view is of a descent, a journey downwards into the depths of the self, to an internal underworld where the laws of everyday reality no longer hold sway: buried within the mind may be both terrors and treasures. Another image is of a journey back in time through the client's memories to her forgotten past; she becomes a 'time traveller', revisiting the scenes of childhood in search of her developmental roots. These spatial/structural and temporal/developmental metaphors are closely linked in psychodynamic thinking: structures are built in layers that parallel developmental phases (see Chapter 2). Both of these journeys – deep into the past and deep into the interior – cover territory which psychodynamic therapy has made its own. It has mapped them in a detail that no other psychotherapeutic theory has: it is often described as 'depth psychology'. In therapeutic work, both types of journey are referred to as regression.

The process of regression

Regression takes place when a person's psychological functioning shifts to a lower level of complexity and differentiation, a less sophisticated form of relating to the world. Developmentally it is likely to appear as the emergence of earlier more childlike states, the reactivation of previous modes of behaviour associated with a prior phase of development.

Feeling 'childlike' at times is a universal experience – a way of representing to ourselves the emergence of these regressive dimensions of our experience. This kind of disintegration of established psychological structures and the sense of reverting to earlier ways of being are common in a variety of ordinary situations: periods of stress or crisis; episodes of illness; being in love; participation in large groups; states of fantasy and dreaming; and episodes of playfulness, creative activity or aesthetic experience (see Chapter 8). In particular, it has been noted that regressions seem common during periods of change or developmental transition. It seems as though in moving out of one established mode of adaptation and into another, people often revert for a time to a less well-organised state. It is in this that the therapeutic potential of regressive experience lies.

The conditions of psychodynamic psychotherapy invite regression, they facilitate a kind of unravelling of a person's usual ways of being. The invitation to free expression removes constraints and conventional accountability and enables surrender to unintegration and dreamlike states. The therapist's permissive understanding of a widened range of thoughts, feelings and behaviour, together with interventions designed to 'uncover' alternative meanings, disrupt conventional ways of thinking about oneself. The therapeutic relationship's security, protection, familiarity and undivided attention and the lack of pressure to attend to the therapist's needs potentiates a parent/child bond which frees the client from 'being responsible' and oriented to external reality. The role of the transference relationship in this process is pivotal: the client's most difficult issues are 'gathered in' to the here and now of the therapy. All these features contribute to a regressive, disorganising dynamism, undermining familiar ways of holding oneself together and dissolving the protective shell that we place around ourselves. They push the therapy towards work at depth.

However, unlike regression that takes place in the ordinary course of life, in therapy it does so in a context which is controlled and limited: the process is made available for reworking and transformation. Why is this induction of a controlled disorganisation a useful thing? The observation of periods of disorganisation preceding significant forward steps in normal development suggests a normal oscillation between regression and progression. Relatively fluid transition states exist in between periods of greater consolidation; to enable movement, current forms of stability must be dissolved to allow their reorganisation. A previous self-limiting form of personal integration must be given up to find a newer, richer and more comprehensive psychological structure. Psychotherapy also oscillates between regression and progression, often consisting of a series of critical periods, moments of stuckness and impasse resolved in moments of crisis where a breakthrough is achieved through the breakdown of the preceding stable but rigid compromises (Leiper, 2001).

Psychodynamic theory also understands this process in historical/developmental terms. Regression is seen as a process of return to states reminiscent of childhood in which there is a recapitulation of key events and relationships from an individual's past. The past might be the route to understanding the sources of a person's pain and the choices they made about how they were able to cope with it. Therapy is thus an invitation to re-enter these moments of distress and to discover their source. Classically, this regressive journey was understood in terms of the uncovering of lost memories, experiences and fantasies from childhood. The key task was reconstruction: a new understanding was pieced together of how the child had experienced key events and relationships. While recovering crucial memories and developing a better elaborated knowledge of our personal past still has a place in psychodynamic therapy, it is currently viewed with greater scepticism. The common wish to understand how we got to be how we are often seems to be a defensive displacement of our anxieties about knowing more fully who we are now. Freud's great case histories are masterpieces of intricate reconstruction, which contributed enormously to an understanding of psychological development, the nature of the internal world and the structure of neurotic symptoms. However, in therapeutic terms, this kind of work is likely to be sterile when what is needed is a kind of re-living of the past in the present. It is necessary not just to remember but to re-experience something of the quality of our earlier life and relationships. We have to take the risk of going further into our pain rather than rationalising and avoiding it in safely familiar ways. The hope is to rediscover the paths of our own development, not merely to understand but to choose a different route, to return to the present with both a wider vision and a new direction.

States of mind and levels of development

In venturing on these interior journeys, psychodynamic therapists are not entering uncharted territory: they can act as guides to their clients because they know the terrain; others have been there before; maps have been drawn. The highly developed theories of different psychoanalytic writers have attempted to understand mental phenomena – particularly regressive phenomena – in terms of both psychological structure and the way it is built over the course of development (see Box 6.1).

Box 6.1 A Developing Picture of Infant Development

Freud framed psychological development in terms of a sequence of 'psychosexual phases' with the Oedipus complex as the pivotal point of early childhood development at about 3–5 years. He considered details of an individual's development prior to this hard to ascertain. As a consequence, he tended to take the earlier phases, particularly the earliest, so-called oral phase, for granted. While he speculated theoretically on the existence of a very early 'primary narcissism' – an initial self-contained state in which the infant was not relating psychologically to the world outside itself – this was of limited clinical utility. All prior development was transformed by being focused through the 'prism' of the Oedipal situation and memory of earlier experiences was unreliable. Consequently, relevant clinical data was unavailable.

Much of this changed with the advent of child analysis in the 1920s. While Freud's daughter Anna followed her father theoretically in developing this area, Melanie Klein was more radical. Undertaking interpretative play therapy with very young children, she developed a detailed, if speculative and contentious, vision of early mental life (see Box 6.2). Out of this, from the 1930s to the 1950s, grew a variety of object relations theories – particularly those of Fairbairn and Winnicott in addition to Klein's. These located the crucial events of childhood in the first year of life and made the 'mother–baby' relationship central to our understanding of human development and of therapy.

Contributing to the clinical and theoretical relevance of these developments was the 'widening scope' of psychodynamic treatment in the 1950s. More therapists were attempting to help very disturbed patients, those with psychotic and borderline conditions whom Freud had considered unsuitable because they were unable to develop well-structured transference relationships. The new theories enabled therapists to cope with these patients through a better understanding of the transferences that they did form.

Finally, building on the work of Bowlby and Mahler in the 1950s, which included direct observation of children from a psychodynamic point of view, a new generation of researchers in the 1970s and 1980s studied the development of very young babies and their modes of relating to their mothers. They demonstrated empirically that infants were capable of quite sophisticated interactions and gave credence to the still disputed idea that the earliest months were formative in subsequent psychological development. In recent years, the observation of infants with their mothers has become widely used in the training of psychodynamic psychotherapists.

Freud's original model of the mind was underpinned by the idea that there were two different forms of mental life – different levels of organisation operating according to different rules – which he called primary and secondary process (see Chapter 2). As we have seen, the nature of primary process means that mental phenomena in the realm of the unconscious take on qualities of strangeness and uncanniness. To reach consciousness, they must pass through a process of translation – of articulation in verbal terms and integration with our normal ways of viewing the world. These different modes of mental life always co-exist: the later, secondary mode forms out of the original primary process but it never displaces it, and we are always engaged with the world in both ways. This fundamental idea of the development of a more 'mature' state of mind out of an earlier one has been built upon by successive generations of psychodynamic theorists. Writers in the object relations tradition have articulated this vision of the unconscious depths of the mind in terms of a detailed picture of the earliest years of childhood. The young child's inner world is structured by as yet undeveloped cognitive and emotional capabilities, which govern the nature of the interpersonal relationships created with its caretakers. A map of modes and patterns of experience as a series of developmental phases is thus established. This suggests a hierarchically structured picture of the mind as a series of layers in which more 'primitive', less sophisti- cated ways of functioning are associated with earlier developmental levels. Problems in the earliest phases of life are consequently associated with more severe psychological disturbances. Under the influence of clinical data and the findings of empirical research with infants, these theories continue to evolve (see Box 6.1). While there is no finally agreed picture, there is a unifying strand: a narrative of increasing separation of the infant from the mother, and its individuation as a unique and progres- sively differentiated subject.

This progressive differentiation of the self from others, and of a sense of objective reality separate from our experience of it, is thought of as deriv- ing from an original 'primary unity', an experiential identity of inner and outer worlds. This is conceptualised as taking place in three broad phases, based on the complexity of the object relationships occurring at that period: these have been termed one-person, two-person and three-person forms of object relationship and so of mental life. We shall briefly outline these fundamental structures and the characteristic forms of experience associated with each one, tracing them backwards from the more familiar, mature forms which are representative of how we normally think about ourselves and others (if not how we always act!) through to the most 'primitive' and archaic levels of mental functioning. Each of these modes of structuring experience are states of mind characterised by distinctive forms of anxiety, defence, relatedness, subjectivity and relationship between the inner and outer worlds.

The triadic, three-person level of internal object relations is associated with a notion of 'ordinary' neurotic conflict and, in theoretical terms, with both the Oedipal situation and Klein's (1935) 'depressive position' (see Box 6.2). As the reference to neurotic conflict suggests, there is a range of degrees of maturity within this level but there is an acknowledgement that in terms of both internal states and interpersonal relationships, conflict and ambivalence are inherent to the human condition and will persist. However, at this level there is a qualitively different possibility of resolving such conflicts because they can be thought about and lived with. This is so due to the creation of a 'third position' (see Chapter 7) which mediates experience, can interpret it and views our internal processes as our own creation: we become 'psychologically minded'. The developmental basis of this is the acceptance of our separateness, an acknowledgement of a reality other than ourselves and a respect for the boundaries of other people. Others (objects) are also subjects – there is a mutual recognition of the similarity of ourselves and others as agents and as self-reflective. This gives rise to the notion of a 'depressive' element in the developmental achievement: guilt and remorse are involved in the ways in which we now understand that we 'use' others. Much will be said about this process in the following chapter. What is clear is that intense feeling states provoke the collapse of this kind of psychological mediation while deprivation or impingement in childhood impede its development.

Box 6.2 Klein's Developmental Positions

Melanie Klein was a pioneer in tracing the foundations of psychological development to the first year of life. She built her theoretical understanding on the basis of Freud's 'dual instinct theory': innate forces that tend towards either life or death. She saw these as operating from birth, giving rise to both strong loving impulses and powerful destructive ones like envy. These impulses are directed towards objects in the environment, such as the mother, or more primitively, 'part-objects', such as the breast. Klein saw mental development taking place through the interplay of 'projective' and 'introjective' processes – the infant attributes internal states to the external object and constructs internal representations of the object related to. However, under the sway of its inherently ambivalent instincts the infant is presented with a terrible dilemma: the object that is loved and needed is also the object that it hates and seeks to destroy. The object, through projection, is then experienced as loving and potentially comforting but dangerously hostile as well.

- *The paranoid schizoid position.* In the first few months of life the only way the infant can cope with the intolerable situation created by its ambivalent instincts is to split both the ego and object-representations into 'good' and 'bad' parts and then to project these separately to create the experience of a good and bad object. The good object can then be idealised and enjoyed but the bad object remains a source of intense persecutory anxiety. This is reinforced by actual frustrations but is fuelled by the infant's own projected destructiveness. Emotional equilibrium is maintained but at the expense of splitting both internal and external reality (the schizoid element) and locating danger and destructiveness outside the self (the paranoid element).

- *The depressive position.* Over the course of the first year the infant becomes more able to appreciate that the mother is a whole person – the need to split her into separate good and bad parts diminishes. This is accompanied by the realisation that the infant's own destructiveness has been directed towards a single object that is also deeply needed and loved. This situation gives rise to anxiety of a depressive nature – the fear of damaging or losing the object as a result of these destructive attacks. Consequently, there may be attempts to protect the object by inhibiting or redirecting aggression, or to make good the damage or integrity of the object through some form of reparatory activity.

Depressive anxieties are mitigated in subsequent development by the existence and introjection of a benign whole object. However, Klein refers to both these periods as 'positions' rather than stages as they have the potential to reoccur or underlie emotional states throughout life. They reflect the origins of the most primitive mental mechanisms, including those which, due to the predominance of unconscious fantasy over reality, are characteristic of psychotic disorders.

At the dyadic, two-person level, the world is composed of subjects and objects but there is no interpreting subject mediating experience. The self is another object rather than the author of its own thoughts and feelings. Instead, these are experienced as forces happening to it. The lack of reflective activity means that experience is ahistorical and meanings are singular. Experience is not 'mentalised'. Instead, it is concrete and absolute. There is no differentiation between the symbol and the symbolised, giving an intense immediacy and reality to all experience. This is the realm of Klein's 'paranoid-schizoid' position (see Box 6.2). While self and other are distinguished, the boundaries between them are fluid and blurred; introjection and projection, splitting and denial mean that parts of the self and the other can be recombined in ways that disregard what belongs to whom. States of the other and the self are experienced as absolutely good or bad and feelings of idealisation, grandiosity, omnipotence, evil, powerlessness and worthlessness structure experience. These states of mind are sometimes referred to as 'psychotic': it is easier to understand delusional, hallucinatory and confusional states if you appreciate the combination of fluidity and absoluteness which characterise this level. However, it is important to recognise that dyadic functioning is prevalent in so-called 'borderline' disorders and also underlies much of what we would normally think of as neurotic problems. In therapy, it creates transference relationships based on 'massive' projections that have an intense and primitive quality. This is the level of functioning revealed in transference regressions.

At the most primitive level of organisation there is what might be called a primal unity, in which there is a lack of differentiation of the most basic categories that define our sense of reality: inside/outside, self/other, past/present, fantasy/reality. Furthest away from ordinary experience, there is perhaps least agreement theoretically about phenomena at this level. Experience of this kind, however, can be understood to form the bedrock of our fundamental sense of what is real. Ogden (1994) calls it the 'autistic-contiguous' level. It is ordered by rhythm and by sensory experience, particularly at the skin boundary. These sensations Tustin (1990) has divided into experiences of softness and fluidity, which she calls 'shapes', and experiences of hardness and edges she calls 'objects'. Such experiences are respectively soothing and defining; they mediate our sense of existing, of safety in space and continuity over time. Such phenomena have no socially established meaning; they are not communicative and precede symbolisation. The infant at this level is not relating to others in an external world but to what Winnicott (1965) called the 'environment mother', the process of being cared for itself. Our most profound anxieties are experienced at this level: they concern survival and identity, archaic fears which Winnicott (1974) termed 'primitive agonies'. There is no organised defence against them, simply states of confusion and terror, experiences of annihilation, de-personalisation, de-realisation and invasion. Much of what underlies psychotic states is experienced in these terms. However, most object relations therapists believe that some apparently neurotic people have made profound 'adaptations' at the foundations of their personality in order to manage issues of this kind.

Therapeutic regression

Although regressive phenomena are at the heart of the psychotherapeutic experience in the psychodynamic tradition, there is a significant degree of ambivalence and of theoretical disagreement about their place and value. Originating in Freud's work, there is a view that regression is essentially a defensive process, a retreat from the challenges intrinsic to development and a return to the illusory securities and gratifications of earlier childhood states. Indeed, psychopathology can be understood from the developmental point of view as fixation at and regression to these early modes of being. Kleinian thinkers elaborate this idea by suggesting that there is an active refusal to develop, based on a profound hostility (or envy) towards more developed, better-resourced adult functioning. Thus psychopathology is not merely fixation (an older version of a normal child) but an active distortion of the capacity for development. This interferes with the person's contact with reality, which would otherwise allow experience to modify unconscious magical thinking.

The therapeutic function of regression is therefore to allow the therapist access to these primitive states of mind and to intervene interpretively to symbolise previously unthinkable experiences, which confuse reality with fantasy, self with other. Undertaken in the context of projective identifications in the transference (see Chapter 5), this is the process of 'containment': the therapist receives, holds, works over and feeds back the projections in a more manageable form. It is crucial in this view that regressive longings and behaviour in the client should not be gratified or indulged. This would rob her of the opportunity to face reality and grow up. The technical stance of the therapist is to maintain rigorous boundaries. This provides the necessary developmental 'gradient' to challenge the regressive defences.

Therapists in the 'developmental deficit' traditions have offered a contrasting view of regression as a developmental opportunity rather than a defence. Rather than focusing on the active and hostile element of refusal in regression, they see as central the need to make emotional contact with the client's underlying vulnerabilities in the context of a new and accepting relationship. Psychopathology is understood here also as a distortion of the process of development operating at archaic levels of the mind. However, the distortion is viewed less in terms of an active refusal to move on, than the perceived necessity to adapt to an inadequate care-taking environment. The individual is detached from an authentic experience of herself and her basic need-states, which were met with unresponsive parenting in the early years. In regression, therefore, it becomes possible to 'get to the bottom of things', where these most primitive fears paralyse the possibilities of growth.

As we have affirmed in previous chapters, it is unhelpful to be trapped at either polarity in this debate. There is surely a dialectical process in which validating the client's spontaneity and protecting the essential privacy of her own experience might alternate with challenging her withdrawal and enabling her to reorganise her experience of forming a safe relationship. Those therapeutic experiences in which regression can be seen as benign rather than defensive stand for the hope of a new form of relatedness; they need not be merely greedy and demanding.

Holding and regression to dependence

Regressions may be quite ordinary, short lived, even fleeting or they may be dramatic, prolonged quasi-breakdowns. During some of these it might be most helpful to suspend interpretative therapeutic activity. By working too hard and insisting that the client also work, we might forestall a more productive entry into less organised states of mind. It may be necessary to tolerate the client's 'delusion' of oneness and merger or simply to survive their expressions of hatred and rage. Balint (1968) describes this as being 'unobtrusive', the therapist letting herself be taken for granted. Winnicott (1965) describes it as 'holding'. Bion's (1970) idea of 'containment' builds on this but implies a more active meaning-making, organising and interpretative form of activity on the therapist's part. Holding is simply the first stage of this: what is offered is the therapist's presence, survival and implicit validation of the client's experience. It is a sense of being understood rather than required to understand. By offering this kind of adaptation to the client through providing secure boundaries, continuity of environment, an empathic space, mirroring and an implicit understanding, the therapist enables the client to 'hand over' her own organising ego-functions, to give up her need to hold herself together rigidly.

These experiences may touch on the most archaic levels of psychological life, in which there is very limited appreciation of the differentiation of self and other. Holding mimics the very earliest object relationships prior to the process of separation. The therapist is experienced as a background presence – like Winnicott's 'environment mother'. This level of mind is pre-symbolic and words are of limited usefulness. Verbal interpretations are likely to be experienced as intrusive or demanding, experiences which repeat an original lack of attunement. Bollas (1987) suggests that the kernel of 'ordinary regression' is silence – it permits an aimless, musing state of mind in the client, lingering over random sensations, unconnected thoughts, a kind of profound free expression of an inward nature, releasing the mind from all normal organising activity. There is an evocation of the deepest parts of the self and a potential for realisations of new meanings that come unbidden. Bollas sees this as contributing to the client's self-analysis, giving space for the discovery and acceptance of the self as it is.

However, holding is relevant to various forms of regressive experience – particularly rage – and not only to this dependent state. The therapist must understand and accept the client's need for her to be present and attuned – sometimes just to survive – and not introduce a different perspective. Without this, a productive regressive experience might be foreclosed or turned in the direction of some breakdown or acting out. The client must be 'met': failure to do so is likely to be based on interference from the therapist's countertransference anxieties. The therapist needs to be able to give up her own defensiveness towards these primitive existential fears, to face experiences of annihilation and yet retain her sense of identity in order to maintain a presence, connected to the client's regression but at the right distance. The provision of such an intersubjective context of holding is at the heart of facilitating this kind of creative regression.

Box 6.3 Case Example – Part 4: Going Deeper

The therapist used her understanding of her own reactions to identify further patterns of potential enactment with Stephen. She gently interpreted the fears she felt he had about her rejecting or withdrawing from him or failing to understand the extent of his suffering. Over the next few months Stephen became less focused on his external problems but moved in and out of states where he felt profoundly dead and empty inside. He was terrified of these experiences but was reluctant to speak about them for fear that they would be overwhelming both to himself and the therapist. One night he had a vivid dream in which he was working in a Victorian mansion, cleaning shoes and scrubbing the floor in a candle-lit basement room. The lady of the house came in. She appeared to be his mother but she didn't acknowledge him as her son. She complained of his waste of candles and snuffed them out leaving him to continue working in complete darkness. He awoke terrified by the dream and felt increasingly suicidal as the day progressed.

In their next session he thought the therapist was cold and out of touch with him and glossed over the dream. However, when she commented on the terror of being left alone in a dark and empty space he began to tremble and felt a desperate and painful longing inside. He admitted that he felt completely out of touch with other people and thought there was a vacuum inside him that could not be filled. The therapist was deeply moved by his profound distress but did not actively try to intervene or reassure him. Although it was hard to remain with him in this painful state of mind she tried to maintain an attentive and responsive presence and ended the session on time despite a temptation to extend it.

This session set the pattern for what followed over Christmas towards the end of the first year of therapy. Stephen became more and more connected to feelings of inner emptiness and futility while at the same time he talked more and more openly about previously unexamined aspects of his early childhood and his most intimate relationships. For example, he recalled that as a child his mother had been unable to look after him after the birth of his brother and that he had been sent to his grandmother who lived nearby and was effectively cared for by her for the next two years. The arrangement ended when he was five after his grandmother had a stroke. He then returned home and was told by his mother that he would need to be her helper, a role that he actively took up.

Although Stephen was periodically deeply distressed he managed his various responsibilities adequately. He was often tearful at home but found his wife was more sympathetic than previously. The therapist took care to maintain the consistency and boundaries of the sessions and Stephen began to appreciate the holding framework that the therapy offered him without needing to see the therapist in such a positive light. He felt he was exposing his most vulnerable side to the therapist but no longer felt he had any choice or control over what emerged.

Risk and regression

There are regressive elements in all helping relationships. This is widely recognised and commonly expressed in terms of the dangers of creating dependency on the helper. The psychodynamic view is that dependency needs are universal but that if these are gratified inappropriately it will be to the detriment of the client's developing maturity. Psychodynamic therapy is in many ways an invitation to regress but this only makes sense in the context of a focus on the person's growth potential. Regression is encompassed in an overall 'adult' setting and its value depends on the client's capacity for tolerating and reflecting on her experience.

Sometimes, rather than having what seems to be a benign quality in which therapeutic potential is easy to identify, regressions take on what Balint (1968) termed a 'malignant' character. These are prolonged destructive episodes in which the client loses the capacity for self-observation and therapeutic responsiveness which is necessary for her to benefit from being in touch with these primitive levels in herself. Such malignant regressions can take several different forms: destructive acting out (such as suicide attempts, violence and life-damaging decisions); delusional transferences and psychotic breakdowns; and intractable dependencies on the therapist. The therapy may be taken over by a client's relentless and intense demands, which can seem like an insatiable craving for the therapist's love. This kind of situation sometimes reaches delusional proportions: grossly unrealistic perceptions of the therapist are formed with the client losing sight of the therapist's essentially professional role; the 'as if' quality of the therapeutic relationship then disappears. These regressions are desperate and self-destructive defences against the emergence of overwhelming anxiety around issues of attachment and personal safety. This suggests some risks if therapists (and clients) have too concrete a view of therapy as replicating a parent/child relationship. Techniques that emphasise the idea of re-parenting are in danger of seducing the client into a false hope that the therapist can make up for what she did not receive in childhood. Intense procedures aimed at producing cathartic breakthroughs of primitive emotion rather than reflection and containment can also be traumatically regressive. Clients are highly suggestible in these archaic areas and so there are risks of therapists creating false beliefs in the guise of discovering hidden, dissociated experiences. Careful therapeutic work, which is courageous in exploring these areas but modest in its claims and patient in its enquiry, is essential to avoid these catastrophes.

Concern about such anti-therapeutic reactions is particularly strong in relation to more disturbed clients. So-called 'borderline' clients, who have fragile self-structures, are – by definition – particularly prone to regress to primitive states as a habitual response to pain and anxiety. They can seem to lack any concept of a benevolent object and have limited capacities for a reflective internal space. The widening scope of psychodynamic treatment has seen many more of these clients taken on for therapy, with a corresponding increase in experience of dealing with the kinds of challenging regressive behaviour that threaten the viability of the therapy. The likely degree of regression needs to be judged against what the therapeutic framework can manage – the length of time available, the supports systems of both client and therapist and what the therapist feels she is personally able to handle. However, there are always liable to be surprises! The therapeutic strategy can be re-evaluated if the therapist is vigilant to early signs of the client developing an unmanageable regression. Therapeutic technique can be changed to reduce its regressive potential: manifestations can be speedily interpreted rather than allowed to build; transferences should be interpreted and framed in terms of interpersonal patterns rather than unconscious fantasies; face-to-face work reduces the ambiguity of work on the couch; and an active focus on current life issues provides direction.

However, it is by no means always best to 'play it safe'. Experience has suggested that skilled and courageous handling by the therapist can put even very challenging and dramatic transference regressions to therapeutic effect. Disturbances at primitive levels may have to be played out in action with the therapist since they cannot be dealt with initially at a symbolic level. In order to utilise them, the therapist needs to be able to hold her nerve and maintain an attitude of enquiry, staying engaged in the therapeutic relationship while setting appropriate limits to what is tolerable in the client's behaviour and to how much she will 'give' to accommodate the regressive experience. Current thinking increasingly sees a crucial element of malignant regressions as connected to the countertransference responses of the therapist to them. Intense borderline transferences are disturbing to the therapist: powerful feelings of vulnerability, helplessness and rage can be involved, which are difficult to bear. The kinds of impasse found in intractable regressions may, to a significant degree, be due to the therapist's own reactions.

The therapist's regression

As discussed in the previous chapter, there is always a degree of counter-transference participation by the therapist. Particularly in regressive situations, there is a risk that this comes to dominate the relationship, leading to a therapeutic impasse. Balint (1968) notes that during a regression the therapist should maintain a sense of her 'ordinariness' and avoid seeming too wise or powerful. However, just as transference is more massive at these archaic levels, so too is countertransference. The polarisation in the client can profoundly affect the therapist, leaving her feeling powerful, wise and perfect or utterly helpless and useless. She takes on the client's projections, producing feelings of confusion, terror, hopelessness, rage and craziness.

Although these are extreme states, some mutual regression takes place in all therapies. This is unavoidable; in fact, it may be desirable, even essential. Empathy is a kind of mutual regression and the deepest empathy is where the therapist has allowed herself to be gripped and transformed by her relationship with the client. In a sense the therapist has to 'go mad' too: the therapist's capacity to regress in a controlled way is one of her major capabilities. It enables her to tune in to the client's level of organisation while also staying separate and maintaining the working alliance. The therapist, of course, needs the capacity to remain clear about who she is, to maintain her reality testing and independence of judgement free of the client's projections. But such stable boundaries are not enough. She also needs boundaries that are sufficiently permeable for her to use her own unconscious as a tool. Maintaining equilibrium between her capacity to join the client's regression (without maintaining an excessive distance) and her ability to emerge from this to reflect on and organise the experience (without being trapped or gratified) is the aim.

It may be less the fact of being caught in a regression that is potentially destructive than the therapist's inability to deal effectively with it. Ultimately, if the therapist can communicate that she has 'been where the client is' and survived, the client will be strengthened in her capacity to grow. It has long been suggested that the therapist will be unable to guide the client towards areas of growth that she has not experienced herself (Jung 1946/1981). Therapists differ in their tolerance both for regressive behaviour in clients and for the discomfort of regressive countertransferences in themselves. They need to be in touch with and accept their own potential for regression and to be relatively undefended and open to the experience of archaic anxieties. It is when we try to escape the discomfort, say through an excess of organising therapeutic activity, that therapy gets stuck. Unsurprisingly, the image of the therapist who always understands what is going on and remains in control of the therapy at all times is popular with both clients and practitioners. It is in fact a kind of weakness. It may well be, as Searles (1999) suggests, that successful work, particularly in the areas of severe regression, requires mutual emotional growth.

Regression in the service of development

In the traditional view, archaic levels of functioning are as far as possible to be transcended and controlled through the dominance of later and more sophisticated psychological structures: the 'ego' replaces the 'id'. Regression to the less organised levels of the personality is seen as the source of psychological difficulty; primary process functioning is associated with fantasy, illusion and distortion. This vision of maturity is one of rational control and the transformation of the less structured into better organised ways of functioning. However, a less hierarchical vision understands the continuing presence of different ways of ordering experience, each with its own validity, as the foundation of a creative relationship to the world. The archaic levels of our mind bring to experience a power and immediacy without which life would lose passion, depth and intensity. These unconscious elements are the source of our interest and connection with life: they are the source of both creative and destructive potentials. The aim for the therapeutic process becomes a freeing of the capacity to navigate between different levels of psychological organisation, to keep open bridges between them, sustaining an ongoing process of internal integration, which is never complete. The defensive barriers of repression and denial interfere with this exchange and an increased richness of experience and freedom of thought and feeling are promoted by dismantling them. Regression is thus not principally into the past or to the core of the self, but is the opening of internal barriers and the overcoming of constraint within experience. It is not a retreat but an expansion. Through allowing an element of constructive disintegration, new forms of organisation are engendered that are less guarded, less controlled by anxiety and more open to the full range of our experience.

The therapist is a crucial mediator in this developmental process. In managing her own 'regressive' connections to both her own and her client's unconscious, she is able to follow the client at archaic levels of functioning. At the same time she is 'ahead' of her, more able to articulate and to integrate these areas of experience. Her activity is thus constantly modelling the capacity to build bridges between areas of the mind and to organise and give meaning to experience. She mediates a higher level of organisation through her interventions.

Conclusion

In the double vision of regression referred to at the beginning of this chapter, there is what might be thought of as a kind of creative ambiguity. We do not have to resolve whether to think in terms of a developmental/sequential model or a structural/simultaneous one: both are needed. A developmental vision contains an idea of progression and maturity towards which therapy aims. In holding this ideal the therapist can keep in mind the ways in which we all refuse the demands of growing up and cling defensively to what we know and do not want to relinquish – how we need to give something up in order to move on. On the other hand, therapy needs the complexity of a vision that appreciates the ongoing tensions and irresolvable dilemmas at the heart of what is most important to us. This view enriches our sense of human life, gives value both to our pain and conflict and to the primitive dimensions of our experience: creative transformation is continually needed as a response to the unease at the heart of existence. In the process of regression, therapy leads in these twin directions of change: they are respectively differentiation and creation.

Change, it seems, is difficult. What brings people for therapy is the experience of an intractable problem: they are stuck and unable to help themselves. They come with the hope of finding an expert who will know or work out the solution to their problems. Their expectations – sometimes hidden, sometimes only thinly disguised – are often that a kind of magic will take place. But these hopes of an all-powerful healer are to be disappointed. One of the core tenets of psychodynamic change is that it takes hard work.

The effort required has many layers. Of course it involves an investment in each of the processes of change which have already been explored: taking the risk of expressing thoughts freely, being willing to seek new understandings with honesty, committing ourselves to a new intimate relationship, and getting in touch with primitive areas of experience. A degree of courage is required to face the pain involved in each of these processes, but it seems that more might be required. There is an element of sacrifice: some things have to be given up in order to allow us to move on. Familiar ways of securing a sense of safety and old means of gaining satisfaction may have to be relinquished to create space to build something new. Effort is also involved in the persistence required of both therapist and client: giving up the old and building something new both take time. Psychodynamic therapies became progressively lengthier as clinical experience was accumulated (see Box 7.1). Indeed, psychodynamic therapists came to feel suspicious of rapid change which was not based on hard psychological work. It is thought likely to be a defensive manoeuvre – a 'flight into health' or a 'transference cure' – intended to avoid the pain and effort required for real change.

In a sense, this ethos of effort and persistence is based on experience of the difficulties and disappointments of psychodynamic psychotherapy itself. Psychological problems have been found to be tenacious and many changes are ephemeral. Therapists have had to renounce their own misplaced hopes to be powerful magical healers. In place of these they have had to construct a more substantial vision of therapeutic change with goals that extend beyond a release from immediate problems. The ambitious aim is to construct a more solid foundation for the personality.

Therapists hope that their clients will not wish for too much too soon – but neither should they settle for less than they are capable of.

The compulsion to repeat

That change is not easy should come as no surprise. The persistence of patterns of action from the past is, as we have seen, one of the hallmarks of a psychodynamic understanding of human life. When we experience psychological symptoms we are, as Freud put it, suffering from 'reminiscences' – unprocessed experiences that remain alive and influential in the present. We do not recognise that these are linked to the past and repeat them, often without knowing that we are doing so. Where such experiences remain unintegrated with more mature levels of functioning they will be re-evoked by aspects of the present and repeated in ways that are outside conscious control: they have a compulsive quality. The present is replaying the past and the person – by defensively avoiding the roots of the experience – is rendered passive in the face of it.

Some writers in the ego psychology tradition suggest that this behaviour is not solely defensive, that repetition has an active quality in which the individual is attempting to gain mastery of the past (White, 1959). They are, so to speak, trying to 'get it right this time'. Certainly 'passive' repetition constitutes an opportunity in the context of psychotherapy; through analysis of the transference, therapy functions to make repetitions conscious. By converting them from passive into active through insight into their roots, they become available for integration at a higher level of organisation: something new can be made of them and novel resolutions of the unconscious conflicts fuelling the repetition become possible (Loewald, 1980). Resistance in this 'classical' view is resistance to recognition of the unconscious conflict and recollection of the past. However, therapeutic experience suggests that often there seems to be no change after working with this resistance to awareness and the development of apparently valid insight. Therapy frequently runs into a variety of intractable difficulties. In therapeutic impasses, there are long periods of stalemate in spite of correct technique and seemingly accurate interpretation. Longer therapies and follow-up consultations have found that clients who had gained insight and improved symptomatically for a while can then relapse. Puzzling phenomena are encountered such as the 'negative therapeutic reaction', in which accurate interpretations that should have been helpful seem to lead the client to become worse. It has been suggested that such setbacks may even be the norm in therapy rather than the exception (Leiper, 2001). As these problems were uncovered, therapies lengthened, innovations in technique were tried and psychodynamic theory was elaborated to accommodate them (see Box 7.1). There was a gradual realisation that resistance to change might have other, deeper roots.

Box 7.1 Resistance to Change

In the beginning, psychoanalysis was a short-term psychotherapy! Although always intensive (several sessions a week), the expected length of treatment was just a few months. Freud also offered some celebrated brief consultations which could take the form of a walk in the park. Over the next 20 years the period of therapy lengthened considerably. These days, four to five years is considered normal for an analysis or intensive therapy and longer is not uncommon. Experiments with technique started as early as the 1920s with the work of Rank and Ferenczi and have continued ever since to explore ways of reducing these times.

A number of factors contributed to the lengthening of therapy:

- Widening the range of difficulties tackled (from the original hysterical symptoms).
- Increasingly ambitious goals for therapy (from symptom relief to relationship and personality change).
- Concern about maintaining the gains made in therapy (as former patients returned with further difficulties).
- A growing sense of the limitations and difficulties of psychotherapy (with increased experience of therapeutic failure).

All of these reasons are related to the growing appreciation of the place of resistance and its relationship to personality structure. After moving beyond the attempt to overwhelm resistance within the cathartic method, the analysis of a person's defensive patterns became central to therapeutic technique. Interpreting resistance in order to remove the blocks to remembering was the focus of therapy. However, by the 1920s Freud's therapeutic optimism was rather on the wane.

He proposed a new level of resistance, which he termed the 'repetition compulsion'. He regarded this as not simply a resistance to psychotherapy or a defence against painful experience, but as a fundamental conservative feature of mental life. Resistance to change was built into the principles of psychological functioning. He saw the repetition compulsion as one manifestation of his new and highly controversial concept of the death instinct. This reflected an increased attention to the importance of aggression in addition to erotic pleasure in human psychology.

> The death instinct has not been at all popular with most
> subsequent psychoanalytic theorists and only Klein and her
> followers have been able to employ it in ways that genuinely
> illuminate clinical phenomena. Many writers have put the idea in
> the context of the ageing Freud's growing pessimism about
> hopes of improving the human condition. In a late work, *Analysis
> Terminable and Interminable* (1937), Freud expressed great
> caution about the extent of the progress possible in the face of
> our wish not to change and not to know. Subsequent therapists
> have been less convinced of these limitations.

Adhesive attachment

Therapists' wish to help and their sense that the client *can* 'get better' make it easy for them to miss just how much ambivalence there is about change. There seems to be a terror of change itself and an active commitment to the *status quo* that is more than a defence against re-experiencing some dissociated trauma. There is a dislike of the separation involved in giving up old object relationships which Freud (1937) termed 'adhesiveness'. It is this that seems to fuel the compulsion to repeat. Clinically, this is most commonly remarked upon in the confusing and frustrating way in which abused children often remain very loyal to their harmful parents or a battered woman returns to her violent partner in spite of having other options. In therapy this can manifest as a fear and suspicion of the therapist's empathy and a distrust of the offer of herself as a new, good object.

It was a basic theoretical insight of Fairbairn's at the foundation of the object relations tradition that the core of our experience of self is inextricably tied to the relationship to an internal other, derived from our experience of our caregivers (Fairbairn, 1952). Change, in either our sense of identity or our ways of connecting with others, is a threat to the opposite pole of the self–other relationship. Our present modes of relating are an equilibrium created with difficulty in the past; however painful, they were the best we could do in the circumstances. The constraints of these old ways foreclose possibilities of new experience but they are based in an intense loyalty to our familiar ties. Accustomed patterns of behaving are an invitation to particular forms of interacting with others, which consolidate a coherent sense of self in a predictable world. Thus even bad relationships provide a subtle sense of safety and connection that is experienced as sustaining who we are. There can be a profound fear of being cut off, isolated and utterly alone if stereotyped, neurotic ways of relating are given up. This is easier to understand if we recognise that these internalised others are fantasy figures, rather than the real caregivers.

Such relationships are constructed at a primary process level and are imbued with magical qualities, feared and wished for powers. Self and other are inseparable and a threat to one is a threat to the other. Change will be experienced as dangerous if it involves abandoning what we depend on to define our identity.

In addition to the adhesiveness of these self–other relationships, however, it has been argued that there is an unconscious pull towards the primary process level of functioning itself, which fuels the repetition compulsion. The intensity and immediacy of regressive relating are enticing (see Chapter 6) and are hard to renounce: we are reluctant to give up these familiar patterns of gratification. An object that is magically controllable is a temptation, which makes this regressive level of relating very attractive. This draw towards a 'narcissistic' merger with the object has an active, wilful quality: there is an insistence on the old ways in the face of the fear of choosing new, risky relationships with others who are separate and not under our control.

The pull towards fusion and primary process relationships is an aspect of what Freud (1920) called the death instinct. Klein (1957) and her followers have drawn attention to the manifestations of this hatred of separateness in the spiteful and envious attacks made on good objects. The omnipotence of the self is endangered by dependency on another who is experienced as outside its control and it retaliates in a vengeful, destructive fashion. In these circumstances the greater the goodness of the other, the more dependent and more vulnerable becomes the self and the more dangerous is the destructiveness that may be evoked when the dependent needs are frustrated. The degree to which such hate-filled relationships consolidate into repetitively sadistic (or more accurately sado-masochistic) patterns of relating varies greatly between individuals, but it is important for therapists to realise that clients come to therapy not only with 'good intentions' but also with potentially destructive ones. These are experienced as necessary and justifiable (albeit unconsciously) but it is unhelpful to see them as merely a defence against the frustration of benign needs. It is probably wiser to understand them as an aspect of our universal capacity to hate and the attractions of negativity.

Working through

There has often seemed to be a gap between insight and 'cure', when knowing more doesn't seem to help. Theoretically, this has led to an improved conceptualisation of the complex nature of resistance to change. Therapeutically, something more seems to be needed to deal with the compulsion to repeat than the interpretative uncovering of defences. The idea of therapeutic 'working through' was devised to deal with the complexities of the repetition compulsion and the difficulties that lay in the path of change.

Working through, however, has remained a rather vague notion, a general term for the time and energy needed to overcome the tendency to repeat. It points to the need for a client and a therapist to 'do the time' or, as Freud said, 'to wait and let things take their course'. These exhortations, although salutary, are hardly illuminating. What is it exactly that needs 'working through'? Broadly speaking, theorists seem to distinguish two components, which roughly correspond to the two levels of resistance identified as the source of repetition. Working through change requires both elements. At one level, the therapist uses the repetition to help her client 'become conversant' with the resistance: to come to know it with deep awareness, to recognise actions as repetitive patterns by seeing them as the same thing in different contexts and so to elaborate and reconstruct her awareness of herself and her actions. This is largely equivalent to extending the work of discovering new meaning outlined in Chapter 4. However, the implication of the notion of working through is that to successfully master the compulsion to repeat something more is needed. There is an additional affective component to successful change. Freud originally described this in terms of the intensification and catharsis of the underlying unconscious wishes. However, as the preceding discussion of repetition suggests, it may be better to think of it as working towards overcoming the compulsive attraction of the primary process, of tackling the 'id resistance'. Both elements of working through are necessary and go hand in hand, but it is this affective element that points to a vital new aspect of the process of change.

For the opportunity of change to be realised, something like an act of will may be required. Freud refers to this in terms of the client's need to work through 'in defiance' of the resistance. This is very close to the ideas captured in the concept of the 'therapeutic alliance' (see Chapter 5). Therapeutic success depends on arousing in the client a capacity to take heed of a kind of moral appeal inherent in psychodynamic therapy. In part, this lies in the implicit suggestion that it may be possible to see things differently and to try something new – there is an element of active search and experimentation that embodies the will to overcome repetition. More fundamentally, however, this appeal is to take responsibility for your actions and feelings, to regain a sense of ownership of things that have formerly seemed simply to 'happen' to you. As discussed in Chapter 6, the client is in a sense invited, in psychodynamic therapy, to be irresponsible, to engage with her regressive tendencies. But because this takes place within a disciplined therapeutic framework, it points in the direction of taking greater responsibility by placing experience in a wider context of awareness. This movement into a more active position of increased awareness is a developmental achievement, a progression to a higher level of organisation. The client develops an increased capacity for the function of active self-knowing, taking this over from the therapist.

To address this dimension of working through the therapist has to maintain a delicate balance. She implicitly holds the client responsible for her actions but not as a way of blaming her or moralising about her behaviour. Expanding awareness opens up access to new meanings and so to experiencing commitments and choices as actively made even when clouded by self-deception. It is easy for the therapist to attend to what has conditioned her client's ways of being and to neglect the element of active choice in creating and maintaining these patterns. The Freudian propensity to theorise in scientific terms about 'psychic determinism' can obscure this dimension of therapeutic work. It runs the danger of providing the client only with an intellectual rationalisation for her actions rather than as an increased sense of responsibility for her choices past and present. Such interpretations lack the capacity to promote change. There is a contrasting risk of becoming exasperated and blaming the client for not changing, something which must be handled by maintaining a deep understanding and appreciation of the circumstances within which those original choices were made. The therapist's alliance-promoting capabilities – dependability, patience, devotion to the task, acceptance and respect – may be more important than interpretative skill in supporting the client's growing capacity to take responsibility for herself.

There is a further crucial affective element in making this transition, however. It is that something has to be given up in order to attain this new level of organisation: renunciation is at the heart of the process of working through. What has to be left behind are some of the old ways of achieving a sense of security. This opens the client up to facing the pain of her past and the anxieties of the present. An increased sense of responsibility means accepting the unconscious as part of the self, facing the fact that it cannot be got rid of. This awareness of our limitations and our negativity is humbling and disappointing. It involves a loss of self-idealisation. This element of loss means that working through is similar in many ways to the process of mourning and that mourning is at the heart of all developmental change.

Mourning and renunciation

The process of mourning has been extensively investigated since Freud's seminal study of it (Freud, 1917). Its essential qualities have been confirmed repeatedly. It is a process which takes time, passes through different phases in a repetitive and cyclical fashion, and gradually accomplishes certain tasks – painfully and often with effort – so that it makes sense to think in terms of work being done. In the face of a loss, there is a temporary preservation of the psychological relationship with the object, which is only gradually given up in favour of an acceptance of the reality of its absence and the possibility of reinvesting in new commitments. There are phases of defensive denial of the loss and then of painful intensification of the attachment. Detachment comes bit by bit and is likely to be prolonged; the experience of loss is, as it were, divided into manageable elements without a clear ending to this process.

The emotional development that is the outcome of working through can only be sustained at the cost of facing despair and mental pain. This complex inner process can, of course, be derailed by defensive avoidance, denying either the significance of the bond or that the loss has taken place. Such denial is the opposite of mourning and working through, and it is this that can be identified in 'manic' states of mind of all kinds in which there is an inflated experience of self-importance, power and independence. Severe depression is also due to the inability to bear the reality of loss. Here the experienced abandonment is managed by retaining the other as an internal presence, but one that perpetuates recrimination and blame so that there is a vicious cycle of self-attack. These defensive syndromes point to elements of working through loss which are essential to psychological development: these are the crucial roles played in the process of grief and separation by rage, on the one hand, and internalisation on the other.

Ambivalent feelings are always at the heart of the experience of loss. The threat and frustration caused by no longer having access to someone (or something) whom we feel we want and need precipitates a sense of rage. We find ourselves hating the one whom we love. This internal struggle, which of course causes further feelings of guilt and remorse, is at the heart of the pain of mourning. The powerlessness and insecurity causes not only feelings of hurt, disappointment and smallness, but also rage, destructiveness and envy. The struggle to tolerate these feelings, to contain such ambivalence, is precisely what Klein refers to as the 'depressive position', and it is a key developmental achievement (see Box 6.2). It is essential to sustain the acknowledgement that the object is truly lost to us even though we still love it and that this love predominates over the rage and hatred that we direct towards it. It is possible to be reconciled to the loss through forgiveness and efforts towards reparation, but only if we have faced our own powerlessness and rage. We do not free ourselves from this experience of destructive aggression but learn to live with it without giving in to it. In the Kleinian view, this is a central struggle, which repeats itself over and over again as we deal with the inevitable separations, frustrations and disappointments that are part of life.

Psychodynamic psychotherapy is well known for the strictness, even rigidity, with which it maintains certain kinds of formal boundary. The timing of the beginning and end of sessions is precise; there is a fierce commitment to the regularity of sessions; breaks in the sequence, such as holidays, are well signalled, and attended to. The therapeutic posture is also quite highly boundaried, with a tradition of limited personal availability and a suspicion of being responsive in ways that might be gratifying. This hyper-boundariedness is not maintained solely for ethical or practical reasons, although these are factors. It is also a technical device that subtly focuses attention on the issues of separateness and limitation. The therapist implicitly as well as explicitly maintains a discipline that communicates a refusal – or at least a limit – to indulging the client's wish to be rescued, not to be responsible for herself, not to be a separate adult individual. It inevitably arouses anxieties about separateness, feelings of helplessness and rage, as well as grief and longing. Through marking limits in these ritualised ways, the stage is set for discovering the characteristic ways in which the client deals with these hopes and fears in the transference and for working through the process of mourning once again so as to move the developmental process on. Inevitably, these issues will be re-evoked when the therapy itself comes to an end.

Loss and the Oedipal situation

Classically in psychoanalysis, the model for facing and accepting loss during development has been the Oedipal situation (see Chapter 2). Although reference to this has become a cliché, it is all too easy to overlook or misunderstand the significance of what is at stake in the situation that faces the child in Freud's vision of this stage in growing up. She is being required to give up sole and permanent possession of a parent (for simplicity's sake, it is easiest to think of the mother). This is an enormous loss and a heavy blow to the child's sense of omnipotence. The other parent – say the father – stands in the way, prohibiting access and laying his own claim. In effect, he demands recognition of the legitimacy, indeed the very existence, of a relationship between the parents independent of the child, something that she had hitherto not been capable of being aware of. In doing so, the father enforces the presence of boundaries in the world, the difference between generations and between genders: the child is required to acknowledge who is who. Of course, in reality this is all exceedingly complex: it is happening in two directions at once with both father and mother (or whoever might represent the presence of competing loved figures); both are rivals and objects of desire simultaneously; while the contributions of individual personality, relationships, other parties such as siblings and the impact of culture, circumstances and events are crucial. These losses, if they are not tolerated, can lead to profound feelings of persecution and envy, and set up a sense of grievance and self-denigration. The resolution of the psychological situation lies in relinquishing the unrealistic claim to privileged 'ownership', acceptance of the parental relationship and toleration of the pain that this causes. Relinquishing the exclusive relationship with someone who remains present promotes internalisation while the rival/alternative can also be a helper. Through mourning the loss and bearing the pain, self-esteem is increased and a sense of personal security and 'sanity' is enhanced: the child knows where reality lies. The real relationship with the parent remains; only a fantasy relationship has been given up.

The power of the Oedipal paradigm is less in its capacity to analyse and understand individual family dynamics than the way it vividly represents a fundamental element of psychological reality – the recognition of difference – and how this recognition is a developmental achievement, hard won at the cost of a painful renunciation. It has been increasingly argued that another conceptual model of a key developmental phase, Klein's 'depressive position', is fundamentally similar in the nature of the psychological achievement which is being described. As originally stated, there is a regretful realisation that the mother who was hated and attacked as frustrating is the same as the mother who is loved and needed, and that she would have been damaged by the attacks. Modern Kleinian writers point out that the fundamental recognition at the root of this crisis of conscience is that the mother is separate from the self: she is a 'whole' object in that she leads a life of her own not subject to the infant's omnipotent control. In recognising the hurt and suffering of the mother, the child recognises her mental separateness – that the mother has her own subjectivity, unique and different from the child's. Others are independent of us, not a function of how we want and imagine them to be. Bearing the sense of helplessness and dependency which this realisation gives rise to is a critical struggle and is liable to break down in feelings of envy and jealously. Thus the Oedipal situation and the depressive position are now thought of as essentially the same thing (Britton, 1998; Caper, 1999). Both ways of thinking have value. Both involve renunciation as a crucial developmental process.

Box 7.2 Case Example – Part 5: Pulling Things Apart

As Stephen's therapy progressed into the second year he became aware of his deep neediness for the therapy and became increasingly sensitive to breaks, fearing beforehand that he might not cope and afterwards directly expressing his feelings of neglect. The reality that the therapy would eventually end became more of a concern to him. The therapist linked this to previous losses he had experienced in his life. Stephen started to want to know more about his grandmother and father and began to differentiate his feelings of grief for each of them. He also became aware of his sense of lifelong abandonment, together with real sadness at his lack of present contact with his mother and brother.

The therapist began increasingly to draw attention to the way his own deep sense of neediness played itself out in patterns of behaviour that could actually contribute to pushing other people away because of the unconscious pressures he put on them. Although he at first accepted this interpretation, he eventually became overtly angry with the therapist for failing to understand him. The therapist pointed out that he was angry because she was not 'completely understanding' even though she was offering him an understanding that might be useful to him.

The issue recurred time and time again in different forms with Stephen becoming more overtly impatient with his therapist and with his wife at home. Then Stephen arrived at one session smiling sheepishly. He had erupted at home and had spent the weekend rowing angrily with his wife. They had never rowed so intensely; even after her affair he had just expressed his hurt. To his amazement the weekend had ended not in disaster, as he kept imagining, but in reconciliation, with his wife showing real affection towards him for the first time since the baby had been born. She said it was a relief to find that he was not always so innocent and that she could actually be really furious with him without feeling guilty.

From this point Stephen began to see how he often disguised his resentment and turned it into a moral demand on other people to be good to him because he was so hard working and righteous. He found it difficult to hold on to this realisation about his own behaviour and felt rather shamed by it. However, the therapist helped him see how it was connected with his deep sense of unmet needs and hidden sense of entitlement to a perfectly satisfying relationship. This work took most of the second year as Stephen stepped forward and back in coming to grips with the complex and fixed way that he had previously seen himself and related to others.

During this time Stephen became more reflective and curious about his own mental life. He began to take a more detached view of himself and sometimes wondered what his therapist would make of what was happening in different situations. His acute sense of distress came in decreasing waves and was replaced by an increasing sense of robustness. However, his outlook was sober, he didn't underestimate the work that was needed to breath life back into his marriage and find real satisfaction in his work.

Mentalisation and the third position

This critical developmental shift to the recognition of the separate existence of the other is a fundamental differentiation in the construction of our experiential world. It has been described in terms of discovering a 'third position'. The suggestion is that only by having a further 'external' point of view beyond the self and its object, which permits the observation of both, can there be the opportunity for the recognition of difference.

The Oedipal situation, of course, provides a useful paradigm for this idea of a third perspective from which a two-person relationship can be viewed: the child is in an Oedipal relationship but must imagine being observed by another party, her 'rival'; at the same time she is excluded from the relationship between the others and placed in the position of observer. There is thus a differentiation within psychological space which implies developmentally new cognitive capabilities. In observing your relationships, it becomes possible to think about the links between other people; in envisaging being observed, the capacity to see yourself in interaction with others emerges. Thus it may become possible to entertain another view of a situation while retaining your own, and to reflect on your actions while continuing to be yourself. Thus the construction of what has been thought of as a 'triangular space' provides a sense of a stable independent reality outside yourself. It also allows the growth of a psychological sense of self: you become more than merely conscious but self-conscious. It is possible to realise that your thoughts and feelings are simply thoughts and feelings rather than properties of the world itself. This differentiation is the key to gaining ownership of, and so responsibility for, our own actions and reactions.

In recent years, this developmental differentiation has been described as the capacity for 'mentalisation' or 'reflective function' (Fonagy et al., 2002). The child acquires the ability to see others as having their own subjectivity – that is, their actions reflect their beliefs, desires, attitudes, hopes, knowledge and plans: they are intentional. The child thus develops an understanding of mental states. This new level of symbolic functioning makes others' behaviour much more meaningful and predictable and the world becomes a safer, more coherent place. Crucially, this is intimately linked to the capacity to label and find meaningful your own experience. A child learns that she has thoughts and feelings and can distinguish these from other perceptions and sensations and can symbolise them as an internal state. They no longer have the same concrete reality as the external world. This gives access to a more modulated self-awareness, which is essential in the development of affect regulation, impulse control and a sense of personal agency.

Differentiation

The developmental achievement, which allows recognition of the other as a subject in her own right, is an essential condition of a full experience of your own subjectivity. Personhood in this intersubjective view is dependent on and constituted by a process of mutual recognition. This is not given but something that must be achieved. In a space which is constituted by the dialogue between two independent subjects, each is validating of the other through mutual recognition. Where there is no experience of the other as a separate subject, they simply serve a 'self-object' function, to use Kohut's (1977) term, that is, they support the coherence of the experience of self but not its self-consciousness or separateness. The inter-subjective space becomes flat, two-dimensional and there is only room for a single version of reality to be entertained. Differing points of view are polarised and collapsed into either identity or opposition. It is a world of dichotomous relationships in which there is a choice between extremes: it's either you or me and we are trapped in a perpetual stand-off. To put this in Kleinian terms, the subject experiences its objects as things which it must control by invading or engulfing them, or else be invaded or engulfed in turn. It is not possible for subject and object to remain sepa-rate and intact with some respectful link between them. In these circum-stances, the repetition of old patterns of relationship is inevitable: there is no space or freedom for something new to be tolerated; a single reality is enforced and endlessly recycled. The polarised, complementary quality of relationships in this space, the rigid, ritualised patterns of repetitive inter-action, and the aggression, even cruelty, which can be uncovered in the way they are maintained, all suggest that they can be characterised as 'sado-masochistic', even when there is no obviously sexual or violent con-tent to the relationships.

Benjamin (1995) suggests that these two forms of intersubjective field co-exist: the experience of the separateness of individual subjectivities and the experience of fusion, as a background presence of self-object con-tinuity, constitute two interdependent dialectically related poles of the intersubjective world. There is an inherent tension in the need for mutual recognition and the need for the other as a reliable self-object. Achieving mutuality requires giving up control, but this is inevitably risky and liable to collapse into an effort to extort validation from the other. However, this is self-defeating and results in an inauthentic and repetitive form of rela-tionship, which fails to recognise and confirm your own experience as an independent subject. We are always faced with the challenge of how to deal with other people without assimilating or being assimilated by them. This can only be done by relinquishing control, giving up the desire for omnipotent forms of security and letting yourself be open to influence and, potentially, disappointment by the other.

Winnicott (1971) describes this in what he calls 'object usage'. There is, he suggests, an element of negation in this search for validation from another: the infant in its attempts at ruthless control, acts aggressively towards the mother and experiences her (in fantasy) as being destroyed. It is necessary for the infant to feel secure enough to take this risk with her own negativity, otherwise she cannot find out that the other (the mother) survives the process of attack and in doing so paradoxically validates not only her own independence and robustness but the infant's too. This participation in the dialectic of negation and recognition, of demonstrat-ing independence of mind and surviving attack without withdrawal or retaliation, is crucial to the process of change through differentiation in the course of therapy.

Differentiation and therapeutic change

To enable the client to differentiate, the therapist has to perform a kind of balancing act. She has to join the client in her way of being, to adapt to it or accommodate it; the client should feel understood and held, rather than assimilated by the therapist's way of doing things. At the same time, the therapist must not be completely assimilated by the client's world-view: while affected by the client's experience, she must also retain a capacity for distance and the ability to formulate it from her own perspective. If the client only feels held, there is no room for real change: there is no source of difference in the relationship and so no differentiation. Both Winnicott and Kohut discuss this process in developmental terms as the infant's experience of the mother's inevitable failures to get it quite right, of not providing the perfectly adapted environment for the infant's needs. Development, then, depends on such maternal 'failure' being within manageable bounds. The child differentiates from the experience of a maternal presence previously experienced as like a merger. It is a process of progressive 'disillusionment'.

In this sense, therapy is both like and unlike other relationships (see Chapter 5). There is a continuous tracking between an inside and an outside point of view. The therapist must go beyond identifying with the client's experience and become a distinct and separate presence in the relationship. She must have a mind of her own which disrupts the pull to unity. She does this by speaking from the 'third position' – one of observation and reflection on the therapeutic process. It is this movement that most effectively conveys the therapeutic reality of her separateness. She communicates an understanding for the client's point of view but is still thinking for herself. Therapy runs into an impasse when this balance is not properly maintained (Leiper, 2001). Either the therapist stays too close and there is not enough difference and challenge, or an excessive distance and difference of perspective causes the breakdown of the alliance or the creation of a pseudo-collaborative conformity in the client, who over-adapts to the therapist's view. Equally, however, progress depends on manageable amounts of therapeutic 'failure'. Sometimes this is located in the client's 'stubborn' reluctance to adapt and change to a wider perspective. But sometimes that failure is very real: the therapist does not stay close enough to the client's experience, imposes her perspective or doesn't understand. Surviving these ruptures and re-establishing the equilibrium of contact and distance, accommodation and assimilation, integration and differentiation becomes essential to the success of therapy. It is achieved through the commitment of both parties. The client's sense that the therapist is persisting in trying to understand is crucial.

This balancing act presents enormous challenges to the therapist. It is likely to be distressing and disturbing to get empathically close to the client's painful experience and to let yourself be affected by it. However, the pull to unity and like-mindedness is very strong. The therapist easily gets trapped in patterns of interaction and ways of seeing the world that are defined by the client's vision. The therapist's sense of freedom collapses and she is imprisoned by the coercive power of the client's situation. There is a need to reopen the space and to sidestep these cycles of deadening repetition, which arise from the old, polarised ways of relating to the world. Where the therapist can hold her balance, she enables a degree of interplay between competing points of view to be introduced (see Chapter 8).

This all requires considerable emotional effort – working through – on the part of the therapist. Deep anxieties are touched in the process. The therapist has to process the client's material at a higher level of psychological organisation but emotionally this depends on a process of internal differentiation and working through in which she has to confront her own countertransference resistance to knowing and to bearing the depressive anxieties involved in the separation. In order to manage this, the therapist needs support for her own sense of separateness in order to bear the sense of responsibility, isolation and limited power which this involves. She is greatly assisted in doing this by having a point of reference outside the immediacy of the interaction. Most fundamentally, this is constituted by her sense of identity as a psychotherapist and the connection that this provides with a wider professional community. This link with a third presence, which is both a valued external context and loved internal object, enables the therapist to maintain her balance, to manage the pull of the client's limiting and repetitive patterns and to support restraint, discipline, reflection and symbolisation. It keeps the relationship 'therapeutic'. In this way psychotherapy is both a reciprocal encounter and one 'triangulated' by a third mediating voice (Hoffman, 1998).

Sustaining disappointment

The process of working through the resistance to change leads to psychological differentiation and the building of new mental structures. Experientially, however, it is a process of loss and mourning. Typically, during therapy there will be periods of regressive merger and holding, of feeling understood, but this always breaks down sooner or later. The client and the therapist have to confront their separateness and difference. Periods of enchantment give way to disillusion as separateness and limitations are faced – hopefully in a manageable way. This is likely to take place with respect to the very hopes and goals which first brought the client to therapy. The paradox of therapy is that these hopes are, in part, rooted in precisely the defensive illusions that the client needs to give up. She may hope for a transformation based on a demanding, idealised vision of how things can and should be. She comes to an expert therapist who is 'supposed to know', someone endowed with special power, the longed-for loving parent. It is proper to the course of therapy for these hopes to be disappointed. It is the very power of these illusory hopes that provides the platform for their renunciation. As therapy develops, the client is gradually able to accept her own – and her therapist's – limitations. This is the real transformation.

There is an important strand in psychodynamic work, stemming from Freud, which emphasises this acceptance of limitation, a confrontation with the inherently unsatisfactory elements of the human condition. The austerity of this vision can be overemphasised in some psychodynamic writings but it is an important counterweight to the pull within any therapeutic endeavour towards being seduced by illusions of comfort and perfectibility. There are limitations and disappointments inherent in any human relationship. To care about another person is not simply to risk dissatisfaction and loss – it inevitably leads to them sooner or later. The hope of avoiding the pain of separateness, which is embodied in the client's attempts to cling and to control relationships or to distance and dispense with others through self-sufficiency, does violence to their full potential. She may discover a more realistic hope in the experience of the therapist's patient efforts to stay separate but in touch.

For the therapist too, disappointment has to be borne. She has to face the limits to her therapeutic ambitions without giving up the effort. It is humbling to realise that your best efforts to understand and help someone change will never be wholly successful, will never get rid of the pain that she has to bear on her own. To be of any use to the client, a therapist has to work through her own illusions and tolerate her helplessness in the face of the reality of human suffering, the uncertainty of her influence and the discomfort of the many occasions in which she finds herself unable to understand. For both parties, a sense of the limitation of the therapy – of what it has not achieved – has to be accommodated and worked through in the process of ending to enable the client to move forward towards the future, one in which she feels more fully responsible for the further development which can take place in her life.

Conclusion

In working through resistance and repetition, giving up the securities of old object relationships, renouncing regressive satisfactions and tolerating differentiation within the therapeutic relationship, the possibility of something new is opened up. This is not solely a matter of the stoical renunciation of illusion in favour of a confrontation with the 'harsh realities' of life. Relinquishing our investment in finding an omnipotent caregiver and final authority permits the exploration of new relationships and different satisfactions – of entering the real world of risk. Tolerating limitations enables the appreciation of the worth both of ourselves and other people – we can stop being so choosy. Giving up perfection permits the flexibility to reclaim ownership of dissociated aspects of ourselves – it allows us to be ordinary, which can be a great relief. Perhaps most crucially, mourning and differentiation clear a space within us for creativity and discovery. This creative space allows us to break out of the stultifying pathologies of repetition. It frees our potential for inventiveness and leaves something always to be desired.

Psychotherapy always implicitly contains an idea of forward momentum. The developmental slant of the psychodynamic perspective tends to emphasise the past, its repetition in the present and the active resistance to change at the heart of so much personal distress. The 'analytic' stance seeks to understand and so clear away these obstructions. But there is also a commitment to promote therapeutic change that leads to the construction of something different from the past: fresh experience, improved quality of relationship, increased depth of feeling, a clearer sense of self. This leaves open an important question: what is it that enables something genuinely new to come into being? Is the removal of pathological disorder, distortion or obstruction enough? Or do we need to recognise the operation of something further – a creative process?

Psychoanalytic ideas have been criticised for pathologising the individual and for ignoring the more constructive and self-actualising potentials of human beings that are highlighted in the humanistic therapies. The psychodynamic approach is certainly not starry-eyed about our creative potential. In fact in many ways it sees our problems and pathologies as complex creations in their own right and views their deconstruction as a necessary prerequisite to the release of more constructive energies. However, it has also led to some compelling and culturally influential theorising about the process and products of personal creativity. This includes those aspects of creativity that are rendered most visible in the sphere of the arts, but it also applies to what it means for the majority of us to live an ordinary but creative life. Creativity is often associated in people's mind with the existence of a special and rare talent and its public recognition in a particular field. This can blind us to the creativity that is inherent in more everyday aspects of living. The socially anxious person, for example, may well recognise the freedom to participate with enjoyment in a meaningful conversation as a significant creative achievement. We have to *make* conversation, *make* friends, *make* love and a whole lot of other things if these are to be experienced as real and rewarding rather than alienating, stultifying or merely repetitive. In doing so we bring something into existence that was not there before and probably could not have been precisely predicted. In fact, the pleasure of creation lies in part in its capacity to surprise us – and surprise is a crucial aspect of the psychotherapeutic process.

Creativity is both a goal of therapy – a vision of its hoped for outcome – and a crucial component of the process of change itself, through the construction of new and richer ways of experiencing the world. In this chapter we will try to convey some of the key psychodynamic perspectives on the nature of creative activity, both in the special case of artistic creation and in the normal development of a creative life. These ideas inform therapeutic practice and promote recognition of the therapeutic encounter as a medium for creative action on the part of both client and therapist. They place creation at the heart of personal change.

The need to create

In many ways, the freedom to be creative in love, work and play can be taken as a paradigm for mental health and personal fulfilment. While psychodynamic therapy does not offer any particular prescription for living, it does view a creative engagement with life as central to well-being. However, the association of creativity with those with special artistic or intellectual gifts frequently seems to contradict this assumption. It is common to equate high levels of creative achievement with a propensity towards personal disorder, even madness. Images abound of the suicidal writer, the paranoid scientist and the tortured artist. There are undoubtedly stereotypes at work in this but surely also an awareness of something telling. Real creativity may require us to be open to the full depths of our experience; as such it carries definite risks and dangers as well as life enhancing benefits. Like psychotherapy itself, the act of creation is not necessarily a comfortable process, but something that can affect us in powerful and disturbing ways.

One of the most prominent but often disputed views about creative activity is the idea that it inherently arises to serve a 'therapeutic' function. The origin of this idea goes well beyond Freud but he certainly added to it through his analysis of the production of art. Freud did not believe psychoanalysis had any claim to be able to evaluate the aesthetic qualities of art, but he believed its content could be analysed to reveal something of its psychological genesis. He approached art much as he approached dreams and saw in finished work evidence of the disguised expression of unacceptable, instinctually derived wishes. Essentially, this drew a parallel between the creation of works of art and the creation of neurotic symptoms – but with the critical difference that the work of art was not disabling or maladaptive but socially valued, indeed highly esteemed. Freud labelled the move away from the formation of symptoms to the creation of something of value as 'sublimation' and saw it as underlying all creative activity, although the concept – what exactly sublimation involves – remains rather mysterious. Many have found Freud's account unnecessarily reductive and even devaluing of art but it has inspired a good deal of subsequent cultural and artistic interpretation (see Box 8.1).

Box 8.1 Psychoanalysis, Art and Culture

Although psychoanalytic theory is derived from clinical experience it has had a mutually enriching interaction with the arts and cultural studies. Freud made many literary allusions and famously used Sophocles' play, *Oedipus Rex*, to formulate his concept of the Oedipus complex. He also turned his critical attention directly to works of literature and art, employing the idea that like dreams and neurotic symptoms they could be interpreted as expressing unconscious wishes in a disguised form. One of the most well-known examples of this was Freud's study of Leonardo da Vinci, in which he examined some of Leonardo's paintings in the light of details about his personal life.

Freud eschewed analysis of the aesthetic properties of art but focused on the sources of its creation and the way it represented unconscious processes. This has led to a tradition of psycho-biographical criticism that has focused on the life of creative individuals. It has also informed the way characters in fiction have been approached and 'analysed'. In contrast to Freud's emphasis on the individual artist, Jung and his followers have utilised the theory of a collective unconscious to explore the common themes and myths that arise across cultures. This approach makes use of the concept of archetypes to approach recurring motifs in art, such as the hero or heroine, good versus evil and the search for wholeness.

Another strand of enquiry has been informed by object-relations theory, in particular the work of Klein and Winnicott. A Kleinian approach to art and aesthetics focuses on the attempt to achieve integration and wholeness through art under the influence of reparative impulses. The profound impact of some works of art and literature can also be considered in this way, which leads to consideration of the processes involved from the perspective of the observer or reader. This has been examined further using Winnicott's ideas about the complex and active interplay of subject and object, for example reader and text, in the 'potential space' provided by different cultural activities and art forms.

Recent literary and cultural theory has been heavily influenced by the work of Lacan and his assertion that 'the unconscious is structured like a language'. His view of the development of the subject revolves around entry into what he calls the 'symbolic order' of language, which he sees as reflecting the 'law of the father'. Meaning and difference become structured by language but are also pervaded by unconscious desire. This re-writing of the Oedipal complex in linguistic terms has provided a basis for the analytic reading and deconstruction of literary texts and has a wide influence on contemporary cultural criticism, including feminism.

Whereas Freud saw creation as an adaptive solution to neurotic tensions, Klein and her followers recast this idea in different terms: it is a means of reducing anxieties about the damage done to the internalised good object under the sway of the primitive processes of splitting and fragmentation. Making a work of art or creating order in some other context is understood as symbolically restoring the integrity of the object and acts as means of 'reparation' for the harm that was felt to have been done in fantasy. This conceptualisation brings creation into a relational context and provides, through the interplay of projective and introjective processes, a paradigm of how creative activity can help to restore the coherence of both inner and outer reality. This reparative act is a crucial developmental step, an outcome of the move to the 'depressive position' (see Box 6.2) in which responsibility is taken and, furthermore, is made real through a specific act of making amends in a symbolic manner. In fact, both Freud and Klein place these concepts, which they use to account for artistic creativity, at the pinnacle of their respective developmental visions. Sublimation or reparation constitute a more mature way of responding to inner conflict than the defences which they supplant. Creativity, it is implied, is indeed the appropriate outcome of personal growth: it is the desirable form for therapeutic change. Both 'mechanisms' involve giving something up (instinctual satisfaction, vengeful aggression) and its transformation into some other, higher form of expression. It is less clear how this transformation takes place. While it is helpful to view the processes of both sublimation and reparation as developmental achievements, they remain processes that are essentially conceived as responses to internal states that require some kind of correction. They are 'reductive' in their conceptualisation of creativity and their approach to therapeutic change. They might both easily be felt to diminish what are thought of as being our highest achievements.

Both these classical accounts of creative activity would seem to provide support for the commonly expressed fear that psychodynamic forms of therapy may actually reduce creativity. If the urge to create is primarily driven by the need to achieve resolution of neurotic dilemmas or primitive anxieties, then it is reasonable to ask whether a successful analysis of these issues might actually remove that capability. This concern reflects the genuine uncertainty many highly creative people feel about the source of their own creativity, as well as indicating the enormous value they attach to it. It is often experienced as coming from 'elsewhere' and, if necessary, they would rather endure suffering than risk losing it. Nevertheless, this points to a limitation of conceptualisations that foreground understanding of creativity as a means of resolving psychological tensions and anxieties. While this may sometimes be the case, it is unlikely to exhaust the scope of creative activity. In practice, when highly creative individuals enter therapy it is often because their creativity is blocked or inhibited in some way. Although usually associated with considerable distress, what they seek may be less an immediate relief from their suffering than the liberation of their capacity to be creatively productive again. Experience of work with such individuals has led others to postulate a more fundamental place for creativity in psychological development and healthy functioning.

Among the first to take this line was Rank (1932), a contemporary of Freud who inverted the latter's perspective by characterising the neurotic as a failed artist! He saw the need to create as primary and viewed its absence or obstruction as the source of pathology. Rank's approach to creativity identified it as an 'inward necessity' which is linked to the need to achieve independence as a person within the context of their acknowledged dependence on others in the social world. This also has some parallels with the ideas of Jung (1934/1981), who saw 'individuation' as a psychological imperative that needed to be consciously pursued through a creative encounter with symbols arising from the unconscious (particularly within the second half of life). In both these accounts there is a striking emphasis on the role of creativity within a progressive developmental process, one that is central to the evolution of the individual and their ongoing relationship to the world.

The creative infant

For Winnicott (1971) creativity is central to psychic life. Unlike Freud and Klein, it is, for him, a primary category in human experience, involved in both the birth of subjectivity and the sense of an objective reality. Working from the dual perspective of infant observation and analytic practice, he focused on the intimate interlinking of infant and mother in a psychological unity at the beginning of life, a relationship which is continuously and progressively negotiated and re-constructed throughout development (see Box 8.2). In an adequate care-taking environment the baby's fundamental needs are promptly met. For example, the experience of hunger leads to a communication of need, which is rapidly responded to with the provision of the breast or bottle. From the baby's non-differentiated point of view, the experience of wanting the breast leads to its arrival, giving the 'illusion' that it has omnipotently created the breast. Although this is an illusion, it is *not* a delusion: the breast did arrive in response to some action on the baby's part. In an objective sense, the baby did actively co-create the arrival of the breast at that moment. Subjectively, this provides a sense that its desires and actions are meaningful, that they have an impact.

Although this sense of creative omnipotence needs to be outgrown, its existence lays the foundation for the development of a sense of self that feels alive and has a capacity to act with creative agency in and on the world. The baby's 'spontaneous gesture' has to be 'met' by the mother. Her reliability and responsiveness is essential to the healthy development of its relationship with others. If, on the other hand, the environment is unresponsive to the baby's authentic needs – say, the mother is too depressed to respond or insists rigidly on her own agenda – the baby may be obliged to renounce its own spontaneous experience in favour of a protective compliance. In the face of repeated experiences of such a failure to be met, this compliance could solidify into the form of a 'false self' that may seem socially adapted but feels inwardly unreal.

Box 8.2 Winnicott's Phases of Infant Development

Winnicott famously said 'there is no such thing as a baby', meaning that the infant can only be thought of as part of a single psychological system formed with its caretaker. The infant's subjectivity – its sense of self – evolves in interaction with this context and does so through a number of stages which Winnicott never spelled out explicitly but are clearly present in his work:

- *Primary maternal preoccupation* during the early weeks enables the mother to be so closely attuned to her baby that they are in some ways not separate beings. The mother can be thought of as an 'environment mother'. This experience establishes a sense of continuity, of 'going on being'.
- *Mirroring* (or object relating) starts the process of the establishment of self through a reflective 'dialogue' (at a gestural level) with the mother, who treats the baby as a subject in its own right, conferring shared meaning on its actions.
- *Transitional relatedness* establishes a paradoxical condition in which objects in the world can be experienced as simultaneously created and discovered, subjective and objective. This is the first real encounter with the otherness of reality but a full confrontation is avoided.
- *Object use* enables the baby to confront the mother's full externality. It involves the fantasised 'destruction' of the mother – her 'survival' then establishes her independent existence. This lays the foundations for the capacity to be alone and to have concern for others as subjects in their own right.

> Development for Winnicott is a dialectic of oneness and twoness, merger and separation. It progressively builds both the self and the other as independent sources of subjectivity, recognising each other and being recognised in turn.

This process of creative development in conditions of 'good-enough' mothering can be traced through the way a caregiver mirrors the baby's state through gaze and facial expression. This interchange has been elaborated in more detail in subsequent observational research which has shown the extent to which babies both initiate and respond in a mutual interplay of sound, gesture and facial patterning (Stern, 1985; Trevarthen, 1999). In such a state of attuned responsiveness, the baby can be said to be finding itself in the mother's face and in her actions. What is 'found', however, is not already there but something which mother and baby have actively to bring into being through their creative endeavours. The child's affective state is reflected back by the mother or other caretaker, indicating a level of empathic atunement to and understanding of how she is feeling. This should be accurate of course, but must also be modulated. In a sense, the caretaker models how to cope with affect but in doing so she provides the basis for the subsequent symbolisation of those internal states. There is thus a link between the transformation of these undifferentiated mental processes by the caretaker and the construction of capacities for self-regulation and symbolisation in the child. This is very much what Bion (1962) meant by containment (see Chapter 6). If the caretaker fails to mirror the infant's mental state accurately or does so excessively, then it will not be able to create a symbolic representation of its own mental state.

What is at stake is the child's developing sense of self and other, something which Winnicott conceived as emerging particularly out of experiences of a special state of subjective experience which he termed the 'transitional area'. In order to bridge the gap emerging in the developing sense of the difference between self and other, the infant enters an area of transitional experience where objects in the environment can be taken up and used in a way that blurs the distinction between their objectively given and subjectively created properties. A transitional object of this kind – perhaps a piece of clothing or a soft toy – is imbued with a vital importance by the infant and we intuitively understand its significance and allow them to make of it what they will. Winnicott says that the adults don't even raise the question of whether it is a reality or a fantasy – we tactfully leave this ambiguous. The illusion is thus dependent on the collaboration of the 'facilitating environment'. This capacity for creative transformation of reality, with its interpenetration of the subjective and objective, lies at the core of a positive relationship with the world, a sense of aliveness and meaning. Without it the child gradually withdraws, either into a world excessively dominated by fantasy or to an over-adapted, rigid and unimaginative sense of reality.

These primary experiences of creativity are subsequently elaborated in the capacity to play with objects and other people in an imaginative way. Playing and creativity are nearly synonymous for Winnicott and it is the extension of this capacity that he saw as the basis for mature adult creative endeavour. This idea has subsequently been taken up in the context of the therapeutic relationship. This can provide a potential space for transitional forms of experiencing in the area between the client and the therapist: the therapeutic encounter offers an opportunity for creative activity. A client may be able to 'play' with various constructions of self and other and so discover the emergence of a new and more meaningful sense of her own reality and ability to have contact with the world. Play and the transitional realm provide an experience of constructing and investing in the 'game' of life. In this sense, we all create the world and ourselves afresh and must continue to do so for them to remain genuinely meaningful.

Thus at the centre of Winnicott's vision is the idea of a dialectical relationship that is fundamental to our experience: the dialogue between self and other, internal and external, unity and separateness. This interplay is the essence of creativity. It is the basis of the ongoing construction – the organisation and reorganisation – of experience, in a continuing dialogue between the objective and the subjective, things and thoughts, the actual and the possible. Donnel Stern (1997) calls this the dialectic of the 'given' and the 'made'. This constitutes a creative compromise: we make something which is given by the conditions of our reality into our own, but in order to do so successfully we must not violate the properties of what was given. We need the givens of the world, to accept their externality and respect their autonomy – this is at the heart of the process of personal differentiation (see Chapter 7). Without this we collapse into a merged, 'psychotic' state. However, as Winnicott's account so vividly represents, we also need the capacity for imagination and spontaneity and to deploy these in a constant effort to synthesise our experience into a coherent and enlivening engagement with the world.

It thus makes sense to talk of our very experience of reality being created rather than merely something that is given and received. This is not simply a way of describing the processes of infant development that Winnicott takes as his model. It is a life-long process, one of the conditions of human existence. Human experience is constructed not out of nothing or without constraints, but in a never-ending dialectic with the world: this is what lies at the root of our subjectivity. Experience in this view does not come 'prefigured' – there is no natural organisation. It is fundamentally ambiguous until we make something of it, until we interpret it. We are constantly categorising, organising and imagining: all perceptions are to some degree constructions. Any novel experience is a creative interpretation. In therapy, what is discovered is not simply uncovered (see Chapter 4). Rather, something that had not previously existed is brought into being – a new form for experience. Change is brought about through the emergence or construction of this new form. New information or fixed biographical memories are not merely recovered but our experience of self and other are worked over and reorganised. And if this is to be a genuinely *creative* endeavour – in the usual sense of that word – they are reorganised at a higher level: what was isolated and unintegrated is connected, made more coherent; there is an increased articulation and integration. Our experience is in a continuously evolving state – we are constantly called on to exercise this creative synthesising capacity. The relationship between the conscious and unconscious mind is a pivotal element of this developmental progression.

The creative unconscious

There is an ambiguity in Freud's thinking about the relationship of the unconscious to the conscious mind. Typically, symbolic manifestations of the unconscious are seen as structured by the primary process but as arising largely from the pressure of drives to overcome repression (see Chapter 2). It is repression in this scheme that actually gives rise to the unconscious; we have no knowledge of certain experiences because they are deliberately excluded from awareness and emerge, as they do in dreams and symptoms, only in disguised ways. This conceptualisation highlights what is done to avoid knowing, but it also reveals how creative the unconscious can be in finding ways to show itself. While this creativity may frequently be influenced by a need to maintain disguise, it may also have a more fundamental source, one inherent in the theory but less often spelled out. If primary process thinking is fundamentally different from the secondary processes of rational logic and discursive language, it is just not possible to think reflectively in primary process terms. Our consciousness is structured in terms of time, place and the difference between one thing and another. Ignore the reality of these distinctions and our thought would become disordered, even psychotic. To enable it to become conscious, primary process thinking has to find a way to be grasped at a secondary process level: it requires a symbolic transformation. Until this is achieved an unconscious experience is unable to enter normal consciousness without at the same time disrupting it.

This suggests that for consciousness to be present some forms of thinking and experience must, by virtue of their nature, remain unconscious unless translated into a form that can be consciously entertained. The unconscious is not exclusively formed by repression but exists as a direct result of a fundamental incompatibility between conscious and unconscious modes of thought. The logical basis of this incompatibility has been examined in some detail in the innovative work of Matte-Blanco (1975, 1988), who has argued, using mathematical analogies, that the principles of logic governing unconscious thinking are consistent in their own terms but incompatible with the conventional rules that govern conscious forms of reasoning. His analysis led him to believe that what distinguished conscious from unconscious thinking was the need of consciousness to establish and maintain relations of 'difference', while what characterised the unconscious was its capacity to unify and treat experience in an 'undifferentiated' way. Moreover, these opposite polarities, which he labelled as asymmetric and symmetric forms of thinking, could exist in combined structures of thought that contained elements of each. These 'thought-forms' might be imagined as existing on a continuum from thinking that is highly asymmetric and differentiated and thus most clear to consciousness, through to structural forms that are profoundly symmetric and undifferentiated, which would inevitably be deeply unconscious. Undifferentiated structures of thought are actually equivalent to emotional or feeling states, not the abstract kind of thought we usually associate with thinking in words. Thinking should be seen as embodying feeling as well as ideas. This means that contact with emotional experience is fundamental to the construction of more differentiated forms of verbal thought and experience. This rather abstract theorising sheds light on personal descriptions of the creative process and the way it can take place in the context of therapeutic practice. The unconscious – saturated with undifferentiated emotional experience – is crucial to the act of creation.

Artistic creativity involves precisely this construction of symbols to represent such complex feeling states, giving it relevance as a paradigm of the creative process for those involved in therapeutic work. Foremost among those who have explored this connection in depth is Marion Milner. In a series of detailed explorations of her own creative process in writing and painting, and also through the use of artistic expression by her clients, Milner (1957, 1987) describes the need for a rhythmic oscillation between states of fusion or merger and more detached states of critical awareness. In the former, there is a need to adopt a particular openness to experience in which the distinction between the self and the world can be temporarily loosened, with feelings and images allowed to arise unbidden. In the latter, there is a need to return to a more normal mode of consciousness in which discriminations can be made and critical reworking undertaken. The former state seems to provide the origin of creative and integrative experiences but the latter is necessary to translate them into a communicable – perhaps even fully thinkable – form.

Matte-Blanco's model enables us to conceptualise how this creative process might operate, transforming unconscious experience into forms that are more consciously accessible. Initially, there is a direct contact with a relatively undifferentiated experience that might be felt emotionally or 'seen' in terms of images. This is followed by a process of differentiation, in which the experience is examined and separated out. Then, in turn, some form of reunification occurs, which leads to a more differentiated but nevertheless integrated structural form, such as a more specific image or story. This process requires the active participation of both conscious and unconscious modes of thought with an emphasis that alternates in a cyclical fashion between them. The whole process might move rapidly or go on for some time. It can also become blocked or reach a dead end. However, it holds the potential to result in a significant new creation. In a therapeutic context, this would be the emergence of a new form of experience.

Experience does not become known until it is given form. Prior to that point it remains in Stern's terms 'unformulated', a potential experience but not one we can be said to have had. Stern (1997) thinks of the unconscious as the great repository of unformulated experience. Indeed, in his view they are almost synonymous. In psychodynamic terms, we recognise the existence of experience at an unconscious level but by definition do not know this experience, as it has not acquired any conscious form. For it to become conscious it needs to be represented or formulated in some way. This requires a creative transformation, a process of symbolisation: something else must stand in for it. This could be verbal language or perhaps, some other form of symbolic representation. However, such non-verbal symbols depend on further linguistic transformation for their significance to be more consciously elaborated. This is the basis of the 'talking cure': language actively constructs our conscious experience. A creative use of language, and other forms of symbolisation, is vital to our ability to construct new forms of experience in ways that moves awareness from a potential to a realised form. In doing so it replaces the conventional and clichéd with what is unique and personal.

For therapeutic change, the capacity to enter the undifferentiated state seems particularly significant. Many artists describe the plunge into creative work as intensely difficult and anxiety-provoking. As discussed in Chapter 6, therapeutic change can involve processes of regression to less differentiated levels of functioning and this too entails real risks and difficulties. Regression may be seen as one pole of the dialectic of creation. The process of differentiation described in Chapter 7 is the other. Again the paradigm of artistic creativity is instructive: in order to move forward in creative work there is a constant need to let go of what is unnecessary, pull apart what you have available and to make something new of it. The difficulties inherent in arriving at significant creative transformations are one reason why we recognise real creativity as such an achievement. In therapy, the process of contacting the undifferentiated unconscious demands a willingness to suspend conscious control and to tolerate significant periods of confusion and uncertainty. Undifferentiated experience will be felt before it is understood and can therefore seem terrifying and overwhelming. Alternatively, if the experience is more satisfying, even blissful, it may be difficult to tolerate its renunciation and differentiation into a form that can be related to the conscious realities of life. The act of differentiation contains a destructive element that can give rise to acute anxieties along with an element of loss that must be faced and worked through. Whereas the creative artist usually has to make this journey alone, the therapeutic client has at least one ally to accompany her in the shape of her therapist. She also has a distinctive and unique medium to work in – that formed by the therapeutic relationship.

The creative relational matrix

Although psychodynamic theories often seem to highlight and provide means of understanding what may be seen as 'internal' or 'intra-psychic' processes, its developmental and therapeutic paradigms are, as we have seen, fundamentally relational. What comes into being in the process of the infant's psychological development is the result of an interaction, a creative unfolding that emerges within the matrix formed by self and others. The same is true of the client's progress in psycho-therapy: the matrix of the therapeutic relationship is the essential 'medium' of creative change. Both the client and the therapist construct a shared reality and are in turn constructed by it: their subjectivity – their experience of both self and other – is the product of the inter-subjective processes, conscious and unconscious, taking place in the space between them. This process is dialectical and is unique in some respects to that particular pairing. Ogden (1994) describes this complex co-constructed reality as the 'analytic third'. What emerges from a creative therapeutic relationship is more than the sum of its parts. Both client and therapist participate in the formation of something new that arises from their dialogue.

The therapeutic relationship is made of the same relational 'stuff' as the wider social field but is structured in ways that focus and intensify it, while encouraging the emergence of profoundly personal forms of experience that might otherwise not become known. Its transformative potential lies in placing the intersubjective matrix within boundaries that demarcate a special area. Those boundaries have been likened to the frame of a picture – they help to define and separate what is within the picture from what is outside (Milner, 1987). The frame allows for a combination of things to take place. On the one hand, it enables the 'exposure' of the client's constructive activity in the creation of the problems for which she has sought help and in doing so enables these now conscious intentions and assumptions to be 'deconstructed' and given up (as traced in Chapters 5 and 7). However, these constraints are also crucial to the move towards the wider and more open receptivity associated with creative activity (see Chapter 6). The boundaried but internally unstructured therapeutic framework facilitates, what Coleridge termed in poetry, the 'willing suspension of disbelief': an openness to the emergence of new forms of experience that do not immediately have to make any definite or readily comprehensible sense. Such experience can then be worked on progressively in the protected space provided by therapeutic sessions until new forms of expression or understanding or relationship finally take shape.

As the intersubjective field is deepened and intensified it comes to define and constrain the experience of both parties. It is essential that one of them – usually the therapist – is then able to find a means to 'break the grip of the field', as Stern puts it. This is the 'act of freedom' in the transference discussed in Chapter 5. Often this will be done by putting the experience into words. This move into symbolisation takes them into a new, more fluid space, one which has the creative potential provided by the 'third position' (see Chapter 7) rather than the collapsed dyadic space which had previously gripped them. It becomes possible to imagine alternatives. In order to make this crucial move, both client and therapist may have to search for the right words to capture and elaborate an experience. Associations and images are played out and elaborated in the joint effort to find a form that 'fits' well enough to bring the experience into the realm of what is mutually known. Often this involves a more poetic use and understanding of language than is normal in everyday conversation: the emphasis is on imagery, metaphor and the actual sound of words as conveyors of meaning (Sharpe, 1949). Through this process, experience is 'formulated' in a creative way. But in addition, the process of the search itself is made available to be turned into an internal dialogue, a curiosity and openness to experience on the client's part. She constructs a different internal frame for her experience, in which the dialectic of separateness and union, creation and discovery can find an enlivening and continuously creative role within her future life.

The therapeutic hour is thus, in Winnicott's terms, a 'potential space', a context which facilitates entry into a transitional area of experience in relation to another person. The creative elaboration of such experience does not necessarily require interpretative analysis: Winnicott remarked that a patient's creativity can easily be stolen by a therapist who knows too much. Premature understanding or interpretation can effectively short-circuit the client's own creativity and replace it with the therapist's. Both client and therapist must be able to tolerate and risk uncertainty – they must sustain the potential space for creative work rather than rush to a resolution, for only then will the old frozen positions be overcome and genuinely new forms of experience and relationship be elaborated.

Box 8.3 Case Example – Part 6: Moving Forward

As the second year of therapeutic work came to a close the focus of the sessions became harder to define. Stephen often talked animatedly and yet at other times there were long thoughtful silences which the therapist did not feel she wanted to interrupt. Frequently Stephen would make observations about himself that were simultaneously coming into the therapists mind or would build on things she said and develop them in unexpected ways. The content of what was discussed seemed less concrete and literal but seemed to have many connotations that were followed according to the rhythm of their spontaneous thoughts and the unfolding pattern of the session.

Stephen's appearance had changed. He dressed more casually and had put on a little weight. Despite feeling that he was not working as long hours as he had done previously, he had been offered a promotion at work. This surprised him but he was not sure that it was the right step to take. He had undertaken some independent consultancy work and had really enjoyed this despite his initial anxieties. He was now wondering whether it was time to try his hand at this. It was more varied and interesting than the work he did for his organisation and he was not sure he wanted to take on a greater management role. 'I like being able to come up with creative solutions', he said, 'rather than always having to look after the minutiae'. Nevertheless, he had some doubts about whether he would be in sufficient demand for this to succeed.

His wife was once again pregnant. He spent a long time talking about this in the sessions and was quite clear that it was what he wanted. Even in his darkest moments he had found that he could respond emotionally to his son and was overwhelmed by the love he felt his son gave him. This still made him tearful at times but he said it had made him realise that he too had love to give and that this arose from somewhere deep inside him. His relationship with his wife was more volatile than previously, but was, in his words, 'well and truly alive'.

Stephen had developed a deep appreciation for his therapist and the value of their relationship. He became increasingly aware of what he saw as her idiosyncrasies and was conscious of the subtle differences in her mood without always attributing these to himself. He sometimes teased her for the predictable line she took on certain things and would sometimes say, often correctly, 'I know exactly what you're thinking!' For her part the therapist found the sessions less intensely challenging but engaging and rewarding. She found herself being stimulated to think in different ways and enjoyed the lively to and fro that sometimes occurred.

It was Stephen who prompted the end of the work when he announced his decision to move away from the area to take up an opportunity to become a partner in a small but successful consultancy firm in another part of the country. Therapy was brought to an end over a three-month period, in which the significance of this step was carefully reflected on. Stephen ultimately left with a sense of loss, but also hope and excitement for what the future might bring.

The metaphor of play has often been used to capture something of the quality of this relational activity that carries the process of creative work forward in therapy. The therapist's stance has a sceptical quality towards all the constructions that both she and the client place on their experience of the relationship. This enquiring attitude does not take it all with the deadly seriousness of an absolute reality, but with an 'as if' quality which might indeed be characterised as 'playful'. Ultimately, there is a sense of humour about what they are going through together. But using words like 'play' and 'humour' might convey an impression of a process that is relaxed and light-hearted. This is a misconception. It is the way things are used that characterises play. Words, people and objects can freely stand for more than they appear to be and be used in ways that are inventive and imaginatively involving. The surprising outcomes that this may lead to can give rise to unexpected enjoyment, but the process itself requires intense engagement and a high level of commitment. This may be accompanied by a sense of imaginative flow and freedom but can also feature periods of frustration and futility when things don't come together. Play and humour do not preclude passion and commitment.

In this domain, guidelines on therapeutic practice are of little specific assistance. One of the reasons that there is a large literature on analytic technique is the wish to specify in advance some guidance about what is the 'right' thing to do in any particular clinical situation. This is possible up to a point of course – there is a lot of experience to draw on. But the creative transformation of experience originates in an openness to use what emerges spontaneously in the unique circumstances of each individual encounter. It cannot be pre-determined or scripted in any way. What is required of the therapist is a certain freedom of movement and a willingness to improvise in ways that may seem unusual or surprising. An analogy with musical improvisation points up how the ability to improvise creatively and spontaneously is in fact deeply dependent on the mastery and exploitation of technique: therapeutic discipline is essential in order to be able to go beyond it. Without the reference point of therapeutic principles we have no means of distinguishing creative deviations and original constructions from what is just indiscriminate practice – what Freud feared as 'wild analysis'. However, against the supportive backdrop of conventional method we need to have the courage and the creativity to venture further, guided by our own experience and an imaginative response to the client's needs. When client and therapist are engaged in this way, therapy can be an exhilarating and richly rewarding experience for both participants. They combine to establish a matrix of co-creation to which both can actively contribute and through which both will be changed.

Conclusion

Perhaps it is not really possible to isolate the core of creative activity and see it through only one lens – it is difficult to pin down and retains a certain essentially mysterious quality. Paradox often seems to be central to it and there are limits to what we can put clearly into words. It is less a single process of change than an amalgam of currents that tend towards the synthesising of experience and bringing into existence of something new. In many ways creativity is the antithesis of pathology and a criterion of mental health. Psychopathology freezes experience, locking us into a situation of deadening stasis – it is a failure of imagination. In healthy, creative living there is a constant forward momentum towards new experience, in symptom formation a circular and repetitive reconstruction of the old. This tension, however, seems to lie at the heart of both who we are and what inextricably relates us to everyone else. We must participate in creation in order to come into being and must continue to do so if we wish to remain truly alive. Therapy is often thought of as an attempt to repair what is damaged, but it is better seen as the attempt to bring new forms of experience into being and to cultivate this same capacity in everyday life. As such it is concerned with fostering the ability to live a creative life, to learn from our own lived experience and respond to it in personally meaningful and imaginative ways.

PART III
Contexts and Conclusions

The framework of therapeutic change presented in Part II has focused on the processes of change that take place in the context of individual therapy. We have emphasised how this setting is constructed to favour the development and use of a special kind of relationship between the therapist and client, established within boundaries that set it apart from everyday life. However, the cloistered business of one-to-one psychotherapy does not take place in a social vacuum. It is not possible to shut the consulting room door and just exclude the rest of the world. Both therapist and client bring significant aspects of their immediate and wider social situations into the room and remain embedded in them when they leave. We cannot imagine personal change taking place outside this social context or in isolation from forces that arise there – there is simply nowhere else for it to occur!

The pervasiveness and complexity of family, social, economic and political forces can make the pursuit of change through individual therapeutic intervention seem like a drop in a very wide ocean. Psychotherapy is sometimes criticised for disregarding important social determinants of distress in favour of locating problems, and their solutions, entirely within individuals. On the other hand, it is not uncommon for novice therapists greatly to underestimate their significance in the life of their clients and to be shocked at the forces unleashed within the apparently narrow confines of the therapeutic relationship.

To complicate matters, we are confronted with the reality that the therapeutic enterprise itself is shaped by a whole host of external factors, ranging from political agendas and economic imperatives to professional positioning and organisational requirements. Psychotherapy as we know it is a relatively recently phenomenon that has developed in the particular conditions of the economically developed world in the twentieth century. It has in turn become an intrinsic part of the culture and values of much of western society. Although psychodynamic thinking is at the heart of this development, it has also provided a critical perspective from which the social and cultural dimensions of life can be viewed (see, for example, Box 8.1). Not surprisingly, this has also led to extensions in the practical application of psychodynamic ideas beyond the individual consulting room to work with groups, families and larger social systems.

The impact of the social context on psychotherapeutic activity and the application of psychodynamic ideas to wider contexts of practice are topics that we cannot hope to cover comprehensively in one chapter. However, we will highlight some of the social and contextual issues that are currently relevant to the provision of psychodynamic forms of psychotherapy. In addition, we will briefly outline some of the developments that have extended psychodynamic ideas about change to areas beyond individual therapy.

The context of practice

Although there is a wide range of voluntary forms of counselling, most qualified psychotherapists practice as a means of earning a living. This is an obvious but often neglected fact. Successful practice is dependent on employment within an agency providing psychotherapeutic services or a sufficient supply of clients to be able to work independently. Psychotherapy, like most services, is thus subject to the market forces and economic conditions prevailing in society and to survive has to operate within them. This is probably one reason for the plethora of therapeutic approaches available – markets tend to be exploited by new products even if it is their claims and packaging that most distinguish them. However noble the motives of most therapists, the economic realities of practice cannot and should not be ignored – after all the therapist sets out to gain in a tangible way from her work with clients. Psychodynamic therapy requires a long and expensive training and is usually more extended than other therapeutic approaches. As a result it demands the availability of significant resources in terms of time and money for training to be acquired and for its benefits to be accessed by those in need. Unfortunately, this means that it can be out of practical reach for many who could gain from it.

Access to suitable employment or clients is often mediated by the status of the professional training and membership of practitioners. Although professions always claim to exist to serve and protect the interests of their clients, this is clearly not their only function. Professions also serve the interests of their members, often in direct competition with neighbouring professions. At best this keeps them on their toes but at worst it leads to ideological conformity or even overt forms of restrictive practice. The development of psychoanalysis in the USA is a good example. In spite of Freud's unambiguous view that psychoanalysis should not be viewed as a medical discipline, the American Psychoanalytic Association resisted training of the non-medically qualified until the 1980s. This had a significant effect on the social composition and diversity of the psychoanalytic community in North America for many years and placed psychoanalysis, for good or ill, squarely within the framework of psychiatry. In the UK we are currently seeing attempts by the psychotherapeutic community to regulate practice through legislation that will make registration mandatory for all those offering psychotherapeutic services. Depending on your perspective, such moves are designed either to protect the public by ensuring standards of training and practice or to protect the interests of existing professional groups. It is, of course, possible to see them as both.

While much psychodynamic therapy is practised privately in Britain, there is also limited but increasing provision within the National Health Service (NHS) and through counselling services such as those attached to universities. Provision through an organisational context inevitably brings with it a need for therapists to respond to its specific policy and service objectives, which in the case of the NHS can arise directly from central government. These directives may seem entirely reasonable at one level but are not always easy to reconcile with the processes of therapeutic change we have identified within psychodynamic therapy. One example of this concerns efforts to implement the principles of evidence-based practice (McPherson et al., 2003). This is premised on the entirely logical view that interventions should be evaluated in terms of their effectiveness and that evidence of effectiveness should be central to the choice of what interventions to offer and to whom. A considerable amount of research has been conducted into the effectiveness of psychotherapy, including psychodynamic approaches (Roth and Fonagy, 1996). Most broadly, this indicates that psychotherapy does produce benefits but that it is not easy to discriminate between different models of practice. One consistent conclusion, which is directly in line with psychodynamic expectations, is that the therapeutic relationship is one of the most crucial mediators of change. However, one of the major problems with evidence-based practice from a psychodynamic perspective is that it privileges a bio-medical view of therapeutic interventions in which a standardised treatment is applied to alter a clearly specified disorder or symptom. For this purpose the most reliable way of establishing what works best is to use large-scale, randomised control trials and to compare treatment effects on a statistical basis. In this model, the individual is not the focus of attention – it is the disorders they suffer from that are 'treated' and always in an exactly similar way. This is in complete contrast to the person-specific approach of psychodynamic therapy that usually eschews diagnostic categorisation in favour of detailed individual formulations and interventions that actively harness the personal qualities of individual therapists. Change then becomes a highly individualised process. This makes collective evaluations of outcome of limited clinical usefulness. Notwithstanding these problems, an increasing range of research methods are being applied to psychodynamic forms of intervention. These concern both investigations of outcome (Fonagy, 2002) and the process of change which takes place within therapy (Bornstein and Masling, 1998).

Another area in which organisational demands can conflict with psychodynamic understandings about change concerns the need to control costs. In the case of psychodynamic therapy the most obvious way to try to reduce costs is to reduce the length of the therapeutic work. In fact, many have argued that psychotherapy has a tendency to become unnecessarily extended and self-perpetuating and that there is prejudice in the psychodynamic community against shorter periods of work as being superficial or merely symptom-focused (Molnos, 1995). Longer-term work can also be seen to serve the financial interests of therapists rather than clients. On the other hand, we have seen that psychodynamic processes of change can require time and repeated working through and that short-term improvements are not always long-lasting. A number of people have tried to offer frameworks for brief psychodynamic interventions (for a comparative overview, see Messer and Warren, 1995). These usually rely on identifying an explicit focus – such as a core conflict or relational theme – and tend to involve the therapist being more active in attending to this and challenging related defences. The difficulty arises when management systems, in a bid to control overall costs, seek to specify the length of therapy on a uniform basis or require continuous justification for its extension. This may be an attractive solution in a hard-pressed public health service but has also become a significant issue in the American context of 'managed care' (Kaley et al., 1999). The outcome can be that the necessary commitment to the difficulties and challenges of longer-term work is undermined, with opportunities for lasting change sacrificed to the pressures of short-term economic management.

The individual in society

The relationship between the individual and society has always had a central place in psychodynamic theory even if it has sometimes been neglected in its therapeutic applications. Freud saw the roots of neurosis arising from the inevitable conflict between the desires of the individual and the need for these to be constrained to ensure an ordered society. The internalisation of these social constraints, via the family, is what he thought generates psychological tension and conflict. Later theorising, as we have seen, has focused even more closely on the social and interpersonal context of emotional development, with added emphasis on the fundamental need for such relationship. We are all, in this developmental orientation, fundamentally shaped by our history and our place in a social world.

Our social experience is crucially mediated by the personal qualities of our parents or caretakers but is also situated from birth by major social divisions such as gender, ethnicity, class and religion. We are born into a social position that is constructed in specific ways within society and which may be subject to a variety of forms of inequality and disadvantage as well as diverse forms of cultural richness. One of the problems with any normative model of personal change is that the norms of a particular society may actually be oppressive to the interests of certain groups. Two of the most striking examples of this in the latter part of the twentieth century have concerned the position of women and the gay community. A therapy aimed at achieving social adaptation for a woman or homosexual person in the 1950s might well appear now as a clear reinforcer of the existing social values and an exercise in social control.

The tension between personal freedom and social constraints is played out in a variety of ways in the process of therapeutic change. A client may confront a long-standing sense of personal inadequacy and under-achievement, only to find opportunities to make a desired change through undertaking further education are blocked by the lack of available funding or resisted by powerful pressures concerning gender role or class. The only practical way forward might necessitate a high degree of compromise, but to what extent does personal distress then become an inevitable by-product of such conformity to the prevailing conditions of society?

Many commentators have attributed the changing nature of psychological difficulties to significant changes in society and its cultural values (Marcuse, 1955/1974; Lasch, 1978). For example, Freud's patients at the beginning of the last century were often women whose sexuality could find little room for expression within Victorian double standards. In contrast, many clients living through the consumer revolution of the later part of the century report feelings of meaninglessness and fragmentation in their sense of self and in their relationships – as if nothing is ever satisfying. If social structures and forces are at the roots of distress, it is important to question the extent to which therapeutic work with individuals can really make a difference or whether it is change at a social or political level that is required; for example, through critical movements of social reform, such as feminism and gay liberation, or perhaps through more local forms of community action.

As psychodynamic theory has evolved, certain aspects of it have been criticised for reflecting societal and, in particular, patriarchal assumptions. This is evident in the weaknesses and biases in Freud's theorising about women, and in the formulations of Lacan, in which he equates entry into the symbolic order of society with the 'law of the father'. Some of these ideas appear objectionable and oppressive if understood as universal truths. However, they may also be taken as providing an insight into how prevailing social conditions can be internalised in the complex process of psychological development. The analytic approach does not set out to formulate how things *must* be even if it is sometimes misused in that way. In illustrating how social and personal changes are inextricably intertwined, it offers a potential bridge between the individual and social levels of analysis. This can help to avoid the often sterile and polarised opposition between advocates of personal change and social reform. It is naïve to think that change at an individual level is sufficient to change society, but it is equally unrealistic to think that changes in social conditions will inevitably lead to individual well-being. From a dynamic perspective, these two levels have a far more complex interrelationship.

Entwined in debates about social and personal change is the complex issue of power and its effects (Proctor, 2002). It is not uncommon to hear power discussed as if it were a bad thing, but without it change would not be possible. The effects of power at both a social and a personal level can be harmful but they can also be constructive. In fact, the people who are most vulnerable are generally those without power or who are systematically deprived of it. For psychotherapy to effect change it must have some power to do so, but where is the power derived from and in what direction is it to be used? Indeed, who has the power to decide?

Although power can be seen as a personal attribute, social theorists have also shown how deeply embedded it is in our forms of knowledge and established social structures (Foucault, 1980). People enter psychotherapy with the hope that the therapist has both the knowledge and skills to help them. The therapist's competence to take on this role is legitimated by the authorising power of professional training and qualifications. However, each individual has to accept that role when they enter into therapy and also be willing to assume the complementary role of client. In terms of power, the relationship is nevertheless asymmetrical. The therapist has the established role, accredited knowledge and can 'command' a fee. In psychodynamic work, the client, usually in a state of some need, is required to open herself and become known to the therapist while the therapist's own life remains almost completely undisclosed. Clearly this is a potential recipe for abuse. However, as we have tried to show, it can also provide the initial conditions for significant personal growth and change. Thankfully, few experienced psychodynamic therapists believe they personally possess any special power to change people! However, they do recognise the power of the analytic situation and therapeutic relationship as vehicles for change and usually have confidence in the capacity of their clients and themselves to be able to make constructive use of this. By the end of therapy, the hope is that the balance of power will have become far more equal and that the client will be empowered to negotiate wider changes in her life.

From individual to group therapy

As psychodynamic theory shifted its centre of gravity from drives to an increasing concern with interpersonal relationships, a number of people became interested in the application of an analytic approach to groups. In the UK, this was crystallised during the Second World War in a famous series of experiments in group-based interventions at the Northfield military hospital. This formative period helped set the direction for a number of subsequent advances in the analytic study of groups, the development of group-analytic therapy and the establishment of therapeutic communities.

What has characterised all of these developments is a radical recognition of the social nature of the individual and the potential of using groups to further both personal understanding and to effect change.

Although parallel developments in group work have taken place in other countries and from other therapeutic perspectives, the focus has often remained on the problems presented by separate individuals with relatively little regard to the dynamics and processes that can arise in the group itself. This has been characterised as equivalent to conducting individual therapy in a group situation. The group provides a context for the work and adds something to it in terms of the variety of perspectives and support available, but it is not a primary vehicle for insight or change. To place the group at the centre of the work demands attention to how groups function and the specific phenomena that characterise them. The study of this area requires a move beyond the psychodynamic understanding of the individual to a complementary dynamic understanding of groups, together with the development of methodologies of practice to harness these for therapeutic ends.

One of the pioneers in the psychoanalytic study of groups was Bion (1961). He initiated the first experiments at Northfield and subsequently conducted groups at the Tavistock clinic. He adopted a firmly analytic stance: he didn't try to actively lead or provide any structure for these groups but focused his attention on what unfolded spontaneously in the group-as-a-whole. The results were often highly charged and had a powerful emotional impact on participants. The groups seemed to generate or reveal intense anxieties and often fell into what Bion described as 'basic assumptions' to avoid the challenge of more productive but potentially exposing work. These basic assumptions are characteristic of collective states of mind that can pervade the whole group and temporarily define its purpose. He described three such assumptions in some detail: 'dependency', 'fight–flight' and 'pairing'. For our purposes, the striking feature about these is that they all serve to maintain the group but at the expense of achieving any real change or development. The intense personal anxieties generated by the unstructured group situation lead to group-wide responses which are essentially defensive in nature but which are usually not recognised as such by those who are participating in them.

Bion's work provided a starting point for further exploration of human groups and organisational systems and his example remains influential in the conduct of groups for experiential learning and professional training. However, the use of analytic groups for therapeutic purposes has been most comprehensively developed in Britain through the work of Foulkes and his creation – Group Analysis. Foulkes was one of the first psychoanalysts to run groups and immediately recognised their potential as a medium for therapy (Foulkes, 1948). He identified a number of processes that arise in groups, including those between individual members, directed towards the therapist and with regard to the activity of the group-as-a-whole. For example, transference does not only arise in relation to the therapist but can also occur in a multitude of ways between participants. Drawing on theories from social psychology as well as psychodynamics, Foulkes evolved a distinctive way of working with groups to harness this interpersonal complexity for the purpose of both analysis and individual therapeutic change (see Box 9.1).

Box 9.1 The Practice of Group Analytic Psychotherapy

Psychotherapy groups conducted according to group analytic principles need to be composed and set up to create an optimal group context for therapeutic change. Although there are few restrictions on who can benefit from a group approach, individuals are carefully selected according to their readiness to join a group and with regard to the composition and aims of the group as a whole. Groups can be established around issues that members have in common, for example sexual or alcohol problems, but there are advantages in having a broad mix of people as this provides a diversity of experiences and perspectives for the group to draw on.

Groups usually consist of between six and eight members and may continue with the same membership for a fixed period of time – a 'closed' group – or continue indefinitely with the membership gradually changing as individuals become ready to leave – a 'slow-open' group. Sessions generally last for one and a half hours and usually take place on a weekly basis at a fixed time. A higher frequency of meetings can be used for more intense work and it is also possible to organise a series of groups in more concentrated periods of time as part of a therapeutic programme. Like individual work, the duration, setting and other boundaries of the group are extremely important. There are also group-specific issues, such as any contact between members outside the group, which are highly significant. It is the conductor's responsibility to manage these and to attend to their impact on the group. For example, late coming is not just an individual matter but affects everyone in the group.

The conductor does not seek to lead the group by setting any particular agenda but adopts a receptive 'analytic' attitude towards what is going on in the group. The emphasis is on following rather directing conversation, with attention divided between individual members and their interaction at a group level. An important aim is to encourage active participation in the group and to support the development of the group's capacity to function with increasing autonomy. In this way individuals can come to contribute more and more to the life of the group, not just to meet their own needs but in response to the needs of others and the group as a whole. Slow-open groups have the important added dynamic of an in-built rhythm of change as people gradually leave the group and new people join. This brings issues of loss and change to the forefront and allows them to be frequently re-negotiated as the group evolves.

Group analysis, or group analytic psychotherapy, views the individual as an inherently social being whose difficulties arise and can ultimately only be understood in the context of social life. Just as the relational matrix is the medium of change in individual therapy, the group relational context becomes the medium of change within the therapeutic group. To achieve this the group and its participants need to develop a culture of increasingly open communication and dialogue – a form of free-floating discussion that can be paralleled with free association (see Chapter 3). The therapist's fundamental task is to facilitate this culture in the group, as well as to take and encourage in others a reflective and analytic stance. For this reason, Foulkes saw the therapist as the 'conductor' of the group but not as the only person able to make a therapeutic contribution. He argued that the therapy was undertaken 'by the group, of the group, including its conductor' (Foulkes, 1975: 3). Paradoxically, although it is assumed that the individual cannot be seen in isolation from the group, well-operating groups seem to favour the development of healthy aspects of individuality. They challenge inhibitions and defences which feed personal distress and social isolation. As a result separateness and connectedness develop together dialectically, as they do in successful individual therapies. However, it is necessary for the individual to participate actively in the creation of such a group in order to provide a suitable medium for their own self-creation. In this respect, group analysis brings together the personal and social spheres in a unitary view of what is necessary for change to occur at both levels.

A number of other approaches to group psychotherapy incorporate psychodynamic ideas and principles, alongside group dynamic and other concepts, to fashion their own group-based models of change (for example, Yalom, 1995; Whitaker, 2000). Therapeutic work in groups has also been extended more widely into the development of therapeutic communities where individuals either stay in a residential setting or attend a day-facility on a regular and fairly long-term basis. These settings make use of group therapeutic principles but at the level of shared community living, involving the working through of relational issues on a day-to-day basis, alongside specific exploration in small groups and through other therapeutic modalities (Kennard, 1998). This approach has proved particularly helpful for those with more severe levels of personality disturbance and social difficulties who often fail to respond to more conventional interventions.

Families and organisational systems

Group approaches tend to create a context of therapeutic change that is a closer approximation to the changing social contexts of everyday life than is possible within individual work. The obvious further extension of this is to seek change by working directly with the social groups in which people actually live their lives. One of the primary candidates for this approach is the family, which, as we have emphasised, is considered by psychodynamic theory to be crucially formative of childhood development. Work with children was established early in the history of psychoanalysis by pioneers such as Melanie Klein and Anna Freud, and individual psychotherapeutic work with children continues to this day, often making creative use of the symbolic properties of play to enable analytic work to take place without so much reliance on verbal expression. However, those working with children have often observed how the presenting problem of a child reflects a difficulty within the family as a whole. This often goes unacknowledged but may be pivotal to why the problem has surfaced and be crucial to achieving any lasting change. Such a situation can make resolution of the child's difficulties through individual work alone problematic or even inappropriate.

Family therapy has arisen in part to fill this need and has developed a wide range of models of work stemming from a variety of theoretical orientations. Psychodynamic and group analytic ideas have been one source of influence alongside principles derived from systems theory, structural approaches and more recently narrative conceptualisations. The emphasis in family work has been to view the family as a whole and to make time-limited interventions designed to create changes in the way the family system operates, rather than to establish long-term therapeutic relationships. However, there is evidence of some integration of relational perspectives from recent analytic work into the framework of contemporary family therapy discourse and practice (Flaskas and Perlesz, 1996).

One of the key features of the extension of analytic ideas beyond the domain of individual work has been an effort to integrate psychodynamic concepts with relevant perspectives from other theoretical domains. One of the most challenging developments of this trend has been the extension of psychodynamic methods of study and intervention to even larger social contexts. This includes settings that are created explicitly for the purpose of exploration and personal development, such as dialogue in larger groups (de Mare et al., 1991), but also 'natural' settings that pre-exist within established organisations. For example, Menzies (1970) conducted an influential study of organisational functioning in a large London teaching hospital. She investigated the reasons for the high levels of sickness and turnover among nurses and concluded it was influenced by the way that working practices had developed. These did not seem to be designed to produce effective results or job satisfaction, but more to protect staff from the considerable personal anxieties and responsibilities associated with nursing the ill and dying. Unfortunately, like many defensive manoeuvres, these arrangements did little to actually address the underlying anxieties but directed effort into pointless procedures and policies that served to distance nursing staff from the people they cared for. Thus social systems can actually arise as a form of collective defence against anxiety in a similar way to that outlined by the psychodynamic model of individual conflict. As a result, the organisation can become dysfunctional and increasingly resistant to the need for learning and change. Often the outcome of this is that individuals leave the organisation or break down in some way while the organisation becomes less effective in achieving its purpose.

Psychodynamically-inspired observations of organisational process have been combined with ideas from the field of systems theory (Miller and Rice, 1967; Hirschhorn, 1988) and more recently models of complexity (Stacey, 2001) to generate methods of consulting to business, public sector and voluntary organisations. The focus of these approaches is on the human processes and systems that operate within organisations and which are crucial to their success in the post-industrial world. Change has become ubiquitous within organisational life over recent years and is now seen as a necessity for survival in most areas. The management of change has thus become a key issue for individuals and organisations alike. Alongside psychodynamic insights into individual and collective resistances to change, important contributions have been made in the areas of leadership and the promotion of cultures that allow individuals to be more fully present in their working lives (Hirschhorn, 1998). As organisations demand increasing productivity, they need increasing participation from their staff to be able to respond at all levels to ever-changing circumstances. Once again we find that personal and higher order levels of change are inextricably intertwined.

Conclusion

Change is inseparable from its context and this context is always, inevitably, subject to change. Whether we like it or not we are all products of our time and place and we all contribute to it. This vision may make the process of change seem even more complex and confusing, but it also makes the significance of personal change become potentially more far-reaching. It highlights that the process of change permeates everything and is never-ending. We are part of a complex unfolding, within which we need to construct our own path and pattern of forward transition. In the final chapter we will bring together our vision of this in the context of psychodynamic psychotherapy and beyond.

Psychodynamic theory has changed greatly over time in response to therapeutic experience and its changing intellectual and cultural context. But often it has been slow to do so: in ideas, as in life, there is a reluctance to give up the familiar and move on. Those therapists who have not rebelled against the authority of Freud and distanced themselves from the psychodynamic heritage have often instead clung to his legacy. While this has ensured a stabilising element of continuity, it has also resulted in conceptual confusion and been a brake on innovation. Nevertheless, a wide diversity of ethos and of emphasis has developed which makes it hard to pull together psychodynamic ideas into a single coherent theory of change. Our treatment of this has been to offer a loose integrative framework which holds the diversity within a structure which does not try to coerce agreement with a single vision of change but places different perspectives in some order. In this chapter we review that framework, the kinds of interpretation that may be placed on it and highlight what are, in our understanding, the central features of a psychodynamic approach to change.

The processes of change

Psychodynamic theory has always been drawn to pithy aphorisms that encapsulate the process of change: making the unconscious conscious; removing repression; replacing the id with the ego; a corrective emotional experience, and so on. Catchy as they are, these no longer serve a useful purpose. The complexity of change needs fuller acknowledgement. Its key ingredients cannot be reduced to a single element. There has always been a degree of tension between an emphasis on cognitive insight and the affective process of the therapeutic relationship – the commitment to the therapist's interpretive function and a sense that 'something more' is required. The therapist's presence, actions and tone seem to convey something crucial that her words cannot. Insight needs a context of emotional experience. These are complementary not competing facets of change, but they have too often been polarised. The six-part framework offers a way of breaking down these processes further in order to allow consideration of the differing parts which each might play in the whole therapeutic journey.

Expression starts the process of representing our experience, giving form to it. It is framed within a context that promotes and values a search for a greater level of honesty, openness and emotional freedom. The permissive, receptive atmosphere encourages the unbidden emergence of thoughts and feelings into awareness, placing us in touch with a fuller version of our own experience. As well as communicating something of this to the therapist, it provides an arena for self-reflection and roots the therapy within a personally responsible and reflexive process. The therapist's attention, interest and searching acceptance provide expression with its onward momentum, legitimising and respecting the focus on the content and the process of our own mind.

Understanding is the start of the processes of deeper self-awareness. Grounded in emotional contact with the therapist and consequently with ourselves, new, sometimes surprising, perspectives on our own experience are discovered. The process of looking within is deepened – we look both 'under the surface' and from a different angle. The increasing awareness of our thoughts and feelings and how we position ourselves in relationships promotes the recognition of previously unfamiliar patterns. As we uncover our wishes and fears and the ways that we deal with them, our own role in our difficulties becomes clearer. The therapist's role in prompting this new self-awareness is crucial. Through her enquiring and interpretative comments she promotes the construction and integration of new meaning and provides an implicit model for our own self-reflection.

Relationship with the therapist is pivotal. It is the forum in which re-creations of old relationship patterns can be played out, permitting a deeper form of communication, one that encompasses unconscious experience that is not yet represented symbolically. As these unformulated issues are enacted both parties are likely to get entangled. It is the therapist's responsibility to free the relationship from the net of projections by standing back, finding ways to make sense of what is going on, separating herself from our unconscious expectations and offering new options for relating. The therapeutic relationship constitutes the intersubjective matrix within which all the other processes of therapeutic change can operate.

Regression carries forward the processes of deepening experience. We become immersed in relatively undifferentiated levels of psychological process and may rediscover or relive experiences that seem to stem from earlier in our life. Being in contact with the unconscious and with our vulnerability and dependency expands the sphere of awareness in a way that is only possible through being held by the therapist's background presence. We are enabled to cease doing this mentally for ourselves, thus enabling and sustaining contact with these new areas of our being.

Differentiation moves us out of these merged states of mind and relationship. It is the process of separation, of leaving old securities that depend on fantasy and regressive engagement with the world. We have to give up and mourn the loss of idealisations and omnipotence. We have to face our own and life's limitations. We become more fully responsible for ourselves. This takes time: we have to stick with it, tolerating disillusionment and disappointment while continuing to work at building more mature structures of self-reflection and more realistic forms of identity. The therapist too needs persistence, resilience and the ability to survive the sometimes stormy and unrewarding aspects of this process.

Creation formulates and integrates our experience in new ways. Giving up old securities provides space for the emergence of something new. Higher levels of psychological organisation are achieved which accommodate the painful, previously disowned experience, which the other processes of change have put us more in touch with. We reconstruct our identity in unique, individuated ways. This provides the security to be more open to experiencing ourselves and the world in novel ways. The therapist not only facilitates this, but through recognising these new forms of subjectivity authorises them. There is a sense of a more mutual dialogue being established, an understanding that these new forms of experience are being co-constructed.

These different facets of the change process are summarised in a schematic form in Table 10.1. The issue of whether they are separate processes of change or an intimately linked sequence is something that we wish to leave ambiguous: in a sense they are both, as we shall spell out below. This schema is just one way of articulating the intricate, overlapping processes by which personal change takes place in the psychodynamic arena.

The spiral of change

As this brief summary and overview of the processes of change may have started to make clearer, it is certainly possible to distinguish a central thread or theme running through this way of envisaging the components of psychological change. A narrative sequence can be made of them, the essence of which is a progressive disembedding from previous, relatively undifferentiated and merged states of being. This is not some strict sequential order but a to and fro, a progression that takes place in a spiral of increasing levels of the organisation of experience and the individuation of the self.

The first three elements of this progression are articulated in more classical psychodynamic terms. Expression within the framework of a

Table 10.1 The processes of change

	View of pathology/ focus of change	Aim of change	Client's process of change	Therapist's activity or stance	Potential risk
Expression	Inhibition	Freedom	Representation Communication	Receptiveness Permissiveness	'Dumping'
Understanding	Unconsciousness	Expanded awareness	Insight	Interpretation (uncovering)	Intellectualisation
Relationship	Repetition Projection	New relationship	Transference (resolution)	'Neutrality' (available – separate)	Enmeshment Re-traumatisation
Regression	Superficiality	Depth of experiencing	De-integration	Holding Containment	Breakdown Infantalisation
Differentiation	Merger Dependency	Separateness	Disillusion Renunciation	Resilience	Loss of hope Rupture
Creation	Rigidity Sameness	Spontaneity Agency	Articulation Construction	Curiosity Recognition	Idealisation (of self or therapy)

therapeutic relationship engages the client's experience in a transferrential context, one that is relatively undifferentiated and that is saturated with the unconscious meanings and repetitions from which her suffering derives. The therapist, and hopefully the client, struggle to understand what this means. To do so the therapist needs to find and maintain some separate distance (her therapeutic neutrality) and to formulate the new understandings that arise from that interpretatively. The client needs to face this new version of the 'truth' about herself: it articulates and so expands her self-knowledge, providing a wider range of conscious choice. Doing so thus increases the level of differentiation within herself.

However, this is by no means as straightforward as it first might sound. The client is inevitably embedded in and constrained by the nature of her current experience. She can only hear the therapist's interventions in terms of her existing ways of understanding the world. It is these that become active within the relational field and the therapist is likely to be drawn into this process too. Indeed, if she remains too separate from it, the client's experience does not become fully engaged and a relatively superficial or inauthentic process of change takes place. This places the therapeutic work in an inevitably intersubjective context. The experience of both parties is interdependent. It is perhaps this object relational quality that the final three elements of the spiral are chiefly addressing. Regression is towards the increasing dominance of undifferentiated modes of experience which come to dominate the therapeutic experience and its relational field. Disembedding involves breaking the grip of this intensified transference that the client is mired in and which connects her to archaic undifferentiated levels in herself. This step of differentiation involves giving up the securities of connection with a fantasised magical other. If the first triad of processes endeavours to replace defensive denial with the acceptance of conflict, the second three processes require the client to give up merger and omnipotence in favour of separateness and limitation. But having a mind of her own only becomes a reality through the act – the creative act – of giving new form to experience. The therapist can support this and challenge its absence, but she cannot do it for the client. They struggle together to bring a new form of expressing the client's individuality into being, to break the grip of the field on their minds. But in the end the therapist can only do this for herself. She recognises and so authorises the client's *own* efforts to be more responsible for herself, to be an agent in her own life through creatively giving form to her own unique ways of being.

A dialectical vision of change thus underpins and brings some coherence to these diverse psychodynamic processes. This is the belief that there is a tension between the static and familiar in life and a longing for more, between the relative undifferentiation or interpenetration of past and present, fact and fantasy, self and other, and the possibility of progressively greater clarity, novelty, separateness and articulation of experience. The subjectivities of the client and the therapist are themselves in a dynamic tension that continuously creates the intersubjective quality of the relational field. Such tension (or conflict) is pivotal in any dialectical process. Experience is always seeking but never finding some place of rest and perfect balance. Equilibrium is only preserved at the cost of excluding something, freezing the conflict in some self-limiting posture and blocking further development. Disequilibrium and disorder are the necessary conditions of fertility – they push the demands of the dialectical tension at the heart of experience into the foreground of attention, pressing for a creative resolution. Embeddedness, dependence and the undifferentiated layers of experience are not 'bad', something merely to be left behind. Separateness only makes sense in the context of relationship: differentiation of experience requires its reintegration. In breaking the grip of a frozen interpersonal field through some creative act, the client (and indeed the therapist) expresses her individuality, achieves a higher level of integration but also expresses some new, as yet unarticulated embeddedness in another context: the process starts again. The dialectical spiral of development is an endless one.

The uniqueness of therapeutic processes

Such an overall vision of therapeutic change in development may function in the background to provide an orientation to the work, but any specific therapy is not greatly helped by statements at this generalised level. Indeed, preconceived ideas of what therapy should be are likely to have a stifling impact on its capacity to promote change. In thinking about an individual client, we inevitably think in terms of specific aims and specific processes of change that could move things in an appropriate direction. For therapeutic purposes, therefore, it is more helpful to think of change as multifaceted. Each therapy probably contains several significant change factors: these are not the same in each case, nor can the outcome be reduced to any specific element. Psychotherapy is not a standardised treatment as though for some disease; it has no set course.

All theoretical models of change processes are food for thought. They contribute (perhaps not even consciously) to the therapist's formulations about what might be feasible for an individual, what should be the focus of work, and how this might be approached. But the client's role in this is crucial – what level of work is done and what processes of change are engaged depend on her desire and capacity to use therapy. The therapist's role is dependent on the client's needs, and the client should be the teacher in what these might be. While the client can utilise therapy in various ways, how this works out is also profoundly dependent on the personality of the therapist: how the client can activate her conflicts in the relationship with this individual therapist; how the therapist is able to resonate to the needs and fears of this specific client. Client/therapist matches are a vital but rather poorly understood factor in what change processes are activated in any specific therapy (Kantrowitz, 1996). Our general vision of the therapeutic process proposes that therapist and client will find themselves together in a unique struggle with elements of the intersubjective field that remain unconscious. In the attempt to promote change through freeing themselves from this, there are no standardised solutions.

Along with this more flexible appreciation of the specificity and uniqueness of individual therapies has come a more pragmatic sense of when enough has been done and it is time to end. Idealised accounts of 'criteria' for termination have been replaced with an acceptance that endings happen in various ways. Taking account of life's realities and the role of chance, therapies reach a point where it seems desirable to end rather than an 'end point'. When an individual can probably manage adequately without more therapy or when this therapeutic couple seems to have created as much change as they are capable of for now, dialogue can bring the work to a conclusion. Endings are inevitably incomplete – there is always more to be done. But there is also a further developmental step: while there should be an open door back to the therapist if necessary, the client should also leave with the feeling that she is equipped to make further changes on her own.

Psychotherapy is a unique experience and it can be remembered in very different ways. Sometimes it is vividly recalled as a series of intensely experienced events. On other occasions – often with longer, 'deeper' therapies – it is poorly or vaguely recalled; somehow the whole experience has been internalised rather than being something which happened 'out there'. Often, too, clients recall as particularly influential a few moments, not necessarily dramatic ones, which stick in their minds. Sometimes these are of particular, life-changing interpretations, but frequently they are occasions when the therapist seemed to step out of role, even in minor ways, which were felt to express caring or personal interest, communicating that the client mattered in something more than a professional way. Involvement at a personal, 'unprogrammed' level seems to be crucial.

The place of theory

What, then, is the place of theoretical generalisation within such a therapeutic situation defined by its uniqueness and its live interactive quality? Theoretical models serve a number of functions irrespective of their specific content. They provide an interpretive framework that accommodates and makes more comprehensible and so tolerable the client's often confusing self-presentations. As such they provide a place of 'safety' for the therapist when the going gets tough and underpin her sense of identity, a place from which she is better able to offer a helpful consistency to the client. In a sense, theory means the therapist is not alone. It is a companion linking her to a wider community of colleagues: they are there with her, as it were, thinking about the client too. But she should not hold too tightly to this framework of support. Indeed, the idea of the uniqueness of every therapeutic process might suggest that there is a great advantage in knowing and respecting a variety of theoretical perspectives – not necessarily trying to integrate them but neither seeing them as in competition for the truth. Hoffman (1998) calls this stance 'critical pluralism'. Theory provides a 'reservoir' of possible therapeutic aims, potential understandings and available postures, which the therapist can draw on to imagine what might be optimal in a specific situation. She then has to forego some of the certainties that a specific therapeutic allegiance can provide.

Is there some point at which such inclusiveness should stop? What of other therapeutic styles and traditions? There is certainly a defining sensibility at the heart of the psychodynamic tradition but this is harder to pin down and less helpful to enforce than was once thought to be the case. It is widely appreciated that all psychotherapies share certain common factors – a special relationship, a model and a method that defines the use of the situation, the hope and expectation of change, and, crucially, the client's commitment to the work – but beyond these it should be clear that many other therapies also engage with a similar array of change processes to those that we have listed as central to the psychodynamic approach. They use them in different ways and each tradition creates a unique combination and adds specific elements. The psychodynamic approach is more able now than it has been historically to have a dialogue with these other styles of therapeutic work and to learn from them. However, it also has an enormous amount to contribute to a fuller understanding of all modalities of therapeutic change. The character of our unconscious mental life and the ways in which it comes to infuse interpersonal relationships is a crucial theoretical contribution – it deepens our appreciation of what is taking place in other therapeutic approaches. It has always been clear that psychodynamic therapy is not the best way for every client (or every therapist), but the psychodynamic understanding of change may contribute to other approaches in ways that are useful and enriching to them all.

The psychodynamic tradition has also always reached out towards and formed creative links with other kinds of theory and domains of knowledge. From neuro-psychology to cultural studies, this extensive dialogue and mutual influence continues. These engagements are generative – they contribute to the evolution not only of theory but of therapeutic practice also. For example, recent research in cognitive and developmental psychology is bringing new perspectives to our understanding of therapeutic action through the way knowledge is represented in the mind (Stern et al., 1998). The suggestion is that many crucial events in therapy do not require verbal reflection but involve relational action or 'moments of meeting' that can directly modify implicit structures of knowledge. These and other advances in our ways of understanding continue to challenge and promote development within psychodynamic theory. The tradition's understanding of its own practices and its ways of constructing what these should be continue to change and be elaborated – as they need to do if they are to be true to the values which they espouse for their own practice.

Openness to change

Failures of one kind or another are the source of any impetus to develop – whether personally or theoretically. In a psychodynamic view, personal difficulties, neurotic symptoms or unsatisfactory relationships are not things simply to be got rid of. They contain some new potential for the person; they represent an undeveloped area of the personality which needs to be entered into in order to attain some higher degree of personal integration. But this is a journey in which the destination is intrinsically unclear. In these matters, we seldom find what we set out to discover. A controlling or directive stance – whether by the therapist or the client – endangers the validity of this quest. It stunts its growth and shuts down creative movement.

The key to the psychodynamic ethos, therefore, is curiosity and honest enquiry. This is an ideal that runs deep in a good therapist, and it involves a special kind of uncertainty. The idea of the unconscious, the way that it inhabits us as therapists as well as us as clients, the way it permeates the relational field, rendering our communications inherently uncertain, promotes – or should promote – modesty in the face of what we continue not to know, even when we feel we have made real discoveries. There is always something beyond our present horizon – we should expect to be surprised. This is a severe challenge to our knowingness, something which is not easily given up. Even though psychodynamic theory has for many years espoused the importance of 'not knowing', it too often has done so in rather a knowing way. This streak of rightness – and even righteousness – that is sometimes present in psychodynamic culture runs counter to the best of its fundamental values. In a sense, the psychodynamic therapist has to live in the faith that 'emotional truth' is possible but not attainable: we must aim ourselves towards discovery in order to create a good enough understanding, without needing to believe that we will arrive at some final answer. However we may illuminate things, we simply open further possibilities of questioning. Every answer is an approximation, temporary and correctable.

The fruit of these efforts for our clients and for us, when we in turn enter this role, is a richer experience of ourselves, one that will be unique, although our theories guide and inform what might be hoped for. There is, of course, the discovery that we are a more complex person than we had imagined, that the 'self' that does things and the 'self' that is aware of them are not identical. A greater sense of our own agency may start to arise from this – we are more 'true to ourselves' or feel we have 'a mind of our own'. In opening up the relationship with ourselves, we may also achieve a capacity for a more vivid and passionate relationship with the world and other people. We can manage the perplexing complications of both separateness and connection with greater flexibility and balance. But perhaps the most enlivening way to express these gains is to place them alongside those values that inform the therapeutic task as a whole. We seek an increased willingness and capacity to see things in a new light, to question everyday assumptions, to acquire a greater curiosity and freedom of thought both about the world and ourselves. The aim is the constant evolution of openness towards our experience, liberating our capacity to turn towards what we don't know, to learn from experience and repeatedly to face the mystery of what is beyond our comprehension.

Part I   Change and Psychodynamic Psychotherapy

Bettelheim, B. (1983) *Freud and Man's Soul*. London: Chatto & Windus.
Caper, R. (2000) *Immaterial Facts: Freud's Discovery of Psychic Reality and Klein's Development of His Work*. London: Routledge.
Mitchell, S.A. and Black, M.J. (1996) *Freud and Beyond: A History of Modern Psychoanalytic Thought*. New York: Basic Books.
Symington, N. (1986) *The Analytic Experience: Lectures from the Tavistock*. London: Free Association Books.

Part II   Processes of Change: A Framework

Expression and understanding

Bollas, C. (2002) *Free Association*. Cambridge: Icon Books.
Jacobs, M. (1998) *The Presenting Past: The Core of Psychodynamic Counselling and Therapy* (2nd edn). Milton Keynes: Open University Press.
Lomas, P. (2001) *The Limits of Interpretation* (2nd edn). London: Constable Robinson.
Malan, D.H. (1995) *Individual Psychotherapy and the Science of Psychodynamics* (2nd edn). London: Oxford University Press.
Ogden, T. (1999) *Reverie and Interpretation: Sensing Something Human*. London: Karnac.

Relationship

Casement, P. (1986) *On Learning from the Patient*. London: Tavistock.
Greenberg, J.R. and Mitchell, S.A. (1983) *Object Relations in Psychoanalytic Theory*. Cambridge, MA: Harvard University Press.
Hoffman, I.Z. (1998) *Ritual and Spontaneity in the Psychoanalytic Process: A Dialectical-Constructivist View*. Hillsdale, NJ: Analytic Press.
McDougall, J. (1986) *Theatres of the Mind: Illusion and Truth on the Psychoanalytic Stage*. London: Free Association Books.
Mitchell, S.A. (1988) *Relational Concepts in Psychoanalysis: An Integration*. Cambridge, MA: Harvard University Press.

Regression and differentiation

Balint, M. (1968) *The Basic Fault: Therapeutic Aspects of Regression*. London: Tavistock.

Caper, R. (1999) *A Mind of One's Own*. London: Routledge.

Mitrani, J.L. (1996) *A Framework for the Imaginary: Clinical Explorations in Primitive States of Being*. Northvale, NJ: Jason Aronson.

Mollon, P. (2001) *Releasing the Self: The Healing Legacy of Heinz Kohut*. London: Whurr.

Winnicott, D.W. (1989) *Psycho-Analytic Explorations*. London: Karnac.

Creation

Caldwell, L. (ed.) (2000) *Art, Creativity, Living*. London: Karnac.

Parsons, M. (2000) *The Dove that Returns, The Dove that Vanishes: Paradox and Creativity in Psychoanalysis*. London: Routledge.

Stern, D.B. (1997) *Unformulated Experience: From Dissociation to Imagination in Psychoanalysis*. Hillsdale, NJ: Analytic Press.

Storr, A. (1991) *The Dynamics of Creation*. London: Penguin.

Winnicott, D.W. (1971) *Playing and Reality*. London: Tavistock.

Part III   Contexts and Conclusions

Bornstein, R.F. and Masling, J.M. (eds) (1998) *Empirical Studies of the Therapeutic Hour*. Washington, DC: American Psychological Association.

Chodorow, N. (1999) *The Power of Feelings: Personal Meaning in Psychoanalysis, Gender, and Culture*. New Haven, CT: Yale University Press.

Hirschhorn, L. (1988) *The Workplace Within: Psychodynamics of Organizational Life*. Cambridge, MA: MIT Press.

Messer, S.B. and Warren, S. (1995) *Models of Brief Psychodynamic Therapy: A Comparative Approach*. New York: Guilford Press.

Renik, O. (ed.) (1998) *Knowledge and Authority in the Psychoanalytic Relationship*. Northvale, NJ: Jason Aronson.

Thompson, S. (1999) *The Group Context*. London: Jessica Kingsley.

References

Alexander, F. and French, T.M. (1946) *Psychoanalytic Therapy: Principles and Application*. New York: Ronald Press.

Balint, M. (1968) *The Basic Fault: Therapeutic Aspects of Regression*. London: Tavistock.

Benjamin, J. (1995) *Like Subjects, Love Objects: Essays on Recognition and Sexual Difference*. New Haven, CT: Yale University Press.

Bettelheim, B. (1983) *Freud and Man's Soul*. London: Chatto & Windus.

Bion, W.R. (1961) *Experiences in Groups*. London: Tavistock.

Bion, W.R. (1962) *Learning from Experience*. London: Heinemann.

Bion, W.R. (1970) *Attention and Interpretation*. London: Tavistock.

Bollas, C. (1987) *The Shadow of the Object: Psychoanalysis of the Unthought Known*. London: Free Association Books.

Bollas, C. (1997) 'Interview with Anthony Molino', in A. Molino (ed.), *Freely Associated: Encounters in Psychoanalysis*. London: Free Association Books.

Bollas, C. (2002) *Free Association*. Cambridge: Icon Books.

Bordin, E.S. (1979) 'The generalizability of the psychoanalytic concept of the working alliance', *Psychotherapy: Theory, Research & Practice*, 16: 252–60.

Bornstein, R.F. and Masling, J.M. (eds) (1998) *Empirical Studies of the Therapeutic Hour*. Washington, DC: American Psychological Association.

Breuer, J. and Freud, S. (1895) *Studies on Hysteria, Standard Edition* 2. London: Hogarth Press.

Britton, R. (1998) *Belief and Imagination: Explorations in Psychoanalysis*. London: Routledge.

Caper, R. (1999) *A Mind of One's Own*. London: Routledge.

Ellenberger, H. (1970) *The Discovery of the Unconscious*. New York: Basic Books.

Erikson, E. (1950) *Childhood and Society*. New York: Norton.

Fairbairn, W.R.D. (1952) *Psychoanalytic Studies of the Personality*. London: Routledge.

Flaskas, C. and Perlesz, A. (eds) (1996) *The Therapeutic Relationship and Systemic Therapy*. London: Karnac.

Fonagy, P. (ed.) (2002) *An Open Door Review of Outcome Studies in Psychoanalysis* (2nd edn). Available from: International Psychoanalytical Association.

Fonagy, P., Steele, H., Moran, G., Steel, M. and Higgitt, A. (1991) 'The capacity for understanding mental states: the reflective self in parent and child and its significance for security of attachment', *Infant Mental Health Journal*, 3: 200–17.

Fonagy, P., Target, M., Gergely, G. and Jurist, E.L. (2002) *Affect Regulation, Mentalization and the Development of the Self*. New York: The Other Press.

Foucault, M. (1980) *Power/Knowledge: Selected Interviews and Other Writings, 1972–1977*. New York: Pantheon.

Foulkes, S.H. (1948) *Introduction to Group Analytic Psychotherapy*. London: Heinemann.

Foulkes, S.H. (1975) *Group Analytic Psychotherapy: Methods and Principles.* London: Maresfield.

Freud, A. (1936) *The Ego and the Mechanisms of Defence.* London: Hogarth Press.

Freud, S. (1900) *The Interpretation of Dreams, Standard Edition* 4/5. London: Hogarth Press.

Freud, S. (1905) 'Fragment of an analysis of a case of hysteria', *Standard Edition* 7: 7–124. London: Hogarth Press.

Freud, S. (1910a) 'Leonardo da Vinci and a memory of his childhood', *Standard Edition* 11: 59–138. London: Hogarth Press.

Freud, S. (1910b) *'Wild' Psycho-analysis, Standard Edition* 11: 219–30. London: Hogarth Press.

Freud, S. (1912) *The Dynamics of Transference, Standard Edition* 12: 97–108. London: Hogarth Press.

Freud, S. (1914) *On the History of the Psycho-analytic Movement, Standard Edition* 14: 7–66. London: Hogarth Press.

Freud, S. (1917) *Mourning and Melancholia, Standard Edition* 14: 243–60. London: Hogarth Press.

Freud, S. (1920) *Beyond the Pleasure Principle, Standard Edition* 18: 7–66. London: Hogarth Press.

Freud, S. (1923) 'Two encyclopedia articles', *Standard Edition* 18: 234–62. London: Hogarth Press.

Freud, S. (1933) 'New Introductory Lectures on Psycho-analysis', *Standard Edition* 22: 7–184. London: Hogarth Press.

Freud, S. (1937) *Analysis Terminable and Interminable, Standard Edition* 23: 216–54. London: Hogarth Press.

Greenberg, J.R. and Mitchell, S.A. (1983) *Object Relations in Psychoanalytic Theory.* Cambridge, MA: Harvard University Press.

Hartman, H. (1958) *Ego Psychology and the Problem of Adaptation.* New York: International Universities Press.

Hedges, L.E. (1983) *Listening Perspectives in Psychotherapy.* Northvale, NJ: Jason Aronson.

Hinshelwood, R.D. (1997) *Therapy or Coercion: Does Psychoanalysis Differ from Brainwashing?* London: Karnac.

Hirschhorn, L. (1988) *The Workplace Within: Psychodynamics of Organizational Life.* Cambridge, MA: MIT Press.

Hirschhorn, L. (1998) *Reworking Authority: Leading and Following in the Post-Modern Organization.* Cambridge, MA: MIT Press.

Hoffman, I.Z. (1998) *Ritual and Spontaneity in the Psychoanalytic Process: A Dialectical-Constructivist View.* Hillsdale, NJ: Analytic Press.

Horvarth, A.O. and Symonds, B.D. (1991) 'The relation between working alliance and outcome in psychotherapy: a meta-analysis', *Journal of Counselling Psychology,* 38: 139–49.

Jung, C.G. (1934/1981) 'Archetypes of the collective unconscious', *Collected Works of C.G. Jung* (Vol. 9.1). Princeton, NJ: Princeton University Press.

Jung, C.G. (1946/1981) 'The psychology of the transference', *Collected works of C.G. Jung* (Vol. 16). Princeton, NJ: Princeton University Press.

Kaley, H., Eagle, M.N. and Wolitzky, D.L. (eds) (1999) *Psychoanalytic Therapy as Health Care: Effectiveness and Economics in the 21st Century.* Hillsdale, NJ: Analytic Press.

Kantrowitz, J.L. (1996) *The Patient's Impact on the Analyst.* Hillsdale, NJ: Analytic Press.

Kennard, D. (1998) *Introduction to Therapeutic Communities*. London: Jessica Kingsley.

Klein, M. (1935) 'A contribution to the psychogenesis of manic-depressive states', *International Journal of Psychoanalysis*, 16: 145–74.

Klein, M. (1957) *Envy and Gratitude: A Study of Unconscious Forces*. London: Tavistock.

Kohut, H. (1977) *The Restoration of the Self*. New York: International Universities Press.

Lacan, J. (1977) *Ecrits: A Selection* (Trans. A. Sheridan). London: Tavistock.

Laplanche, J. and Pontalis, J.-B. (1973) *The Language of Psycho-Analysis* (Trans. D. Nicholson-Smith). London: Hogarth Press.

Lasch, C. (1978) *The Culture of Narcissism*. New York: Norton.

Leiper, R. (2001) *Working Through Setbacks in Psychotherapy: Crisis, Impasse and Relapse* (with R. Kent). London: Sage.

Loewald, H.W. (1980) *Papers on Psychoanalysis*. New Haven, CT: Yale University Press.

Lomas, P. (1994) *Cultivating Intuition: An Introduction to Psychotherapy*. London: Penguin.

Mahler, M.S., Pine, F. and Bergman, A. (1975) *The Psychological Birth of the Human Infant: Symbiosis and Individuation*. New York: Basic Books.

Malan, D.H. (1979) *Individual Psychotherapy and the Science of Psychodynamics*. London: Butterworth.

Marcuse, H. (1955/1974) *Eros and Civilization*. Boston: Beacon Press.

Mare, P. de, Piper, R., and Thompson, S. (1991) *Koinonia: From Hate through Dialogue to Culture in the Large Group*. London: Karnac.

Martin, C. and Holloway, W. (2002) 'Personal therapy: like life, it's what you make it'. Paper presented at the Society for Psychotherapy Research UK, Ravenscar, England.

Masson, J.M. (1985) *The Assault on Truth: Freud's Suppression of the Seduction Theory*. London: Penguin.

Matte-Blanco, I. (1975) *The Unconscious as Infinite Sets: An Essay in Bi-logic*. London: Duckworth.

Matte-Blanco, I. (1988) *Thinking, Feeling, and Being*. London: Routledge.

McPherson, S., Richardson, P. and Leroux, P. (2003) *Clinical Effectiveness in Psychotherapy and Mental Health*. London: Karnac.

Meissner, W.W. (1996) *The Therapeutic Alliance*. New Haven, CT: Yale University Press.

Menzies, I.E.P. (1970) *The Functioning of Social Systems as a Defence against Anxiety*. London: Tavistock Institute of Human Relations.

Messer, S.B. and Warren, S. (1995) *Models of Brief Psychodynamic Therapy: A Comparative Approach*. New York: Guilford Press.

Miller, E.J. and Rice, A.K. (1967) *Systems of Organization: The Control of Task and Sentient Boundaries*. London: Tavistock.

Milner, M. (1957) *On Not Being Able to Paint* (2nd edn). London: Heinemann.

Milner, M. (1987) *The Suppressed Madness of Sane Men*. London: Routledge.

Mitchell, S.A. (1988) *Relational Concepts in Psychoanalysis: An Integration*. Cambridge, MA: Harvard University Press.

Mitchell, S.A. (1993) *Hope and Dread in Psychoanalysis*. New York: Basic Books.

Molnos, A. (1984) 'The two triangles are four: a diagram to teach the process of dynamic brief psychotherapy', *British Journal of Psychotherapy*, 1 (2): 112–25.

Molnos, A. (1995) *A Question of Time*. London: Karnac.

Ogden, T. (1982) *Projective Identification and Psychotherapeutic Technique*. Northvale, NJ: Jason Aronson.

Ogden, T. (1994) *Subjects of Analysis*. London: Karnac.

Parsons, M. (2000) *The Dove that Returns, the Dove that Vanishes: Paradox and Creativity in Psychoanalysis*. London: Routledge.

Pennebaker, J.W. (1997) *Opening Up: The Healing Power of Expressing Emotions*. New York: Guilford Press.

Power, M.J. and Brewin, C.R. (1991) 'From Freud to cognitive science: a contemporary account of the unconscious', *British Journal of Clinical Psychology*, 30: 289–310.

Proctor, G. (2002) *The Dynamics of Power in Counselling and Psychotherapy*. Ross-on-Wye: PCCS Books.

Racker, H. (1968) *Transference and Counter-Transference*. New York: International Universities Press.

Rank, O. (1932) *Art and Artist: Creative Urge and Personality Development*. New York: Alfred Knopf (Reprinted: Norton, 1989).

Rappaport, D. (1959) 'The structure of psychoanalytic theory: a systematizing attempt', in S. Koch (ed.), *Psychology: The Study of a Science* (Vol. 3). New York: McGraw-Hill.

Renik, O. (1993) 'Analytic interaction: conceptualizing technique in the light of the analyst's irreducible subjectivity', *Psychoanalytic Quarterly*, 62: 553–71.

Ricoeur, P. (1970) *Freud and Philosophy: An Essay on Interpretation*. New Haven, CT: Yale University Press.

Roth, A. and Fonagy, P. (1996) *What Works for Whom: A Clinical Review of Psychotherapy Research*. New York: Guilford Press.

Rycroft, C. (1979) *The Innocence of Dreams*. London: Hogarth Press.

Sandler, J. (1976) 'Countertransference and role-responsiveness', *International Review of Psychoanalysis*, 3: 43–7.

Sandler, J. and Dreher, A.U. (1995) *What do Psychoanalysts Want? The Problem of Aims in Psychoanalytic Therapy*. London: Routledge.

Schafer, R. (1992) *Retelling a Life*. New York: Basic Books.

Searles, H.F. (1999) *Countertransference and Related Subjects: Selected Papers*. Madison, CT: Psychosocial Press.

Sharpe, E.F. (1949) *Dream Analysis: A Practical Handbook for Psycho-Analysts*. London: Hogarth Press.

Spence, D.P. (1982) *Narrative Truth and Historical Truth*. New York: Norton.

Stacey, R. (2001) *Complex Responsive Processes in Organizations: Learning and Knowledge Creation*. London: Routledge.

Stern, D.B. (1997) *Unformulated Experience: From Dissociation to Imagination in Psychoanalysis*. Hillsdale, NJ: Analytic Press.

Stern, D.N. (1985) *The Interpersonal World of the Infant: A View from Psychoanalysis and Developmental Psychology*. New York: Basic Books.

Stern, D.N., Sander, L.W., Nahum, J.P., Harrison, A.M., Lyons-Ruth, K., Morgan, A.C., Bruschweiler-Stern, N. and Tronick, E.Z. (1998) 'Non-interpretive mechanisms in psychoanalytic therapy: the "something more" than interpretation', *International Journal of Psychoanalysis*, 79 (5): 903–21.

Stone, L. (1961) *The Psychoanalytic Situation*. New York: International Universities Press.

Strachey, J. (1934) 'The nature of the therapeutic action of psychoanalysis', *International Journal of Psychoanalysis*, 15: 127–59.

Sullivan, H.S. (1953) *The Interpersonal Theory of Psychiatry*. New York: Norton.

Symington, N. (1983) 'The analyst's act of freedom as agent of therapeutic change', *International Review of Psycho-Analysis*, 10: 783–92.

Symington, N. (1996) *The Making of a Psychotherapist*. London: Karnac.

Trevarthen, C. (1999) 'The concept and foundation of infant intersubjectivity', in S. Braten (ed.), *Intersubjective Communication and Emotion in Early Ontogeny* (pp. 15–46). Cambridge: Cambridge University Press.

Tustin, F. (1990) *The Protective Shell in Children and Adults*. London: Karnac.

Wallerstein, R.S. (1988) 'One psychoanalysis or many?', *International Journal of Psychoanalysis*, 6: 5–21.

Wallerstein, R.S. (2002) 'The trajectory of psychoanalysis: a prognostication', *International Journal of Psychoanalysis*, 83 (6): 1247–67.

Whitaker, D.S. (2000) *Using Groups to Help People* (2nd edn). London: Routledge.

White, R.W. (1959) 'Motivation reconsidered: the concept of competence', *Psychological Review*, 66: 297–333.

Winnicott, D.W. (1965) *The Maturational Processes and the Facilitating Environment: Studies in the Theory of Emotional Development*. London: Hogarth Press.

Winnicott, D.W. (1971) *Playing and Reality*. London: Tavistock.

Winnicott, D.W. (1974) 'Fear of breakdown', *International Review of Psychoanalysis*, 1: 103–7.

Wolberg, L.R. (1977) *The Technique of Psychotherapy* (3rd edn). New York: Grune & Stratton.

Yalom, I.D. (1995) *The Theory and Practice of Group Psychotherapy* (4th edn). New York: Basic Books.

Index